The New Pub League Quiz Book Number 3

D1328820

The New Pub League Quiz Book Number 3

David Duncan

foulsham

LONDON • NEW YORK • TORONTO • SYDNEY

foulsham

The Publishing House, Bennetts Close,
Cippenham, Slough, Berks, SL1 5AP, England

ISBN 0-572-02460-6

Printed in Great Britain by St Edmundsbury Press, Bury St Edmunds, Suffolk.

Contents

The Pub League Quizzes

The Answers

The Pub League Quizzes

Rules of the Game

These exciting quizzes are taken from the QuizMasters Pub League quizzes. They are great fun to play at home with any number of team members, or you can use the correct pub league rules and try out the quizzes at your local.

If you play in a league, all the games are played on the same day at the same time. Questions are supplied in a sealed envelope to be opened by the question master in the presence of both teams at the beginning of the match. The questions and answers are normally listed together on a single sheet which is only seen by the question master. We have separated them in the book so that a team member can read out the questions, if necessary, when you are playing at home.

TEAMS
Each team consists of four playing members. In addition, a question master/timekeeper is provided by the home team, and both teams supply a scorer (or the team captains can keep score).

RULES
The match is played in two halves. The question master tosses a coin to see who plays first.

The first four rounds in each half are team rounds. There are five questions for each team, which are asked to each team alternately. Conferring is allowed. If the team cannot answer, or answers incorrectly, the question is passed over to the other team for a bonus.

The final round in each half is a round of individual questions. The team which answers first answers the individual questions in the first half, and the opposing team answers the individual questions in the second half. At the beginning of the match, each team member chooses his or her subject for the individual round from the five categories provided. Conferring is not allowed on these questions. If they cannot answer the questions, or answer incorrectly, the questions can be passed over to the other team for a bonus, and all the opposing team can confer.

All answers to the team questions and to bonus questions must be given by the team captains.

TIMING
Thirty seconds are allowed for each answer, which start after the question has been read out. An additional 15 seconds are allowed if the question is passed over for a bonus.

SCORING
All correct team questions: 2 points
All correct individual questions: 3 points
All correct bonus questions: 1 point

The question master acts as the adjudicator and his/her decision is final. If they make a mistake which would result in a question being unfair, they can replace it with one of the reserve questions provided.

Teams use the score sheets provided to keep scores. The scorers check and agree the points after each round. You can copy the score sheet provided for home use.

THE DRINKS ROUND
Questions are also provided for a drinks round. These are not counted as part of the match, but can be used as reserve questions if necessary. There are ten questions for each team, which are asked alternately.

Pub League Quiz Score Sheet

1st HALF	HOME		AWAY	
ROUND 1	SCORE	BONUS	SCORE	BONUS
Q1				
Q2				
Q3				
Q4				
Q5				
TOTAL				
ROUND 2				
Q1				
Q2				
Q3				
Q4				
Q5				
TOTAL				
ROUND 3				
Q1				
Q2				
Q3				
Q4				
Q5				
TOTAL				
ROUND 4				
Q1				
Q2				
Q3				
Q4				
Q5				
TOTAL				
ROUND 5				
Q1				
Q2				
Q3				
Q4				
Q5				
TOTAL				
1st HALF	HOME		AWAY	
TOTAL				

FINAL SCORE: Home Team_____ Away Team_____

2nd HALF	HOME		AWAY	
ROUND 6	SCORE	BONUS	SCORE	BONUS
Q1				
Q2				
Q3				
Q4				
Q5				
TOTAL				
ROUND 7				
Q1				
Q2				
Q3				
Q4				
Q5				
TOTAL				
ROUND 8				
Q1				
Q2				
Q3				
Q4				
Q5				
TOTAL				
ROUND 9				
Q1				
Q2				
Q3				
Q4				
Q5				
TOTAL				
ROUND 10				
Q1				
Q2				
Q3				
Q4				
Q5				
TOTAL				
2nd HALF	HOME		AWAY	
TOTAL				

Pub League Quiz 1

The individual questions are in Rounds 5 and 10 and are on the following subjects: Soccer, Famous women, Name the year, Nature and Spelling.

Team 1

ROUND 1

1 Which formerly warlike tribes of central and southern Sudan are still famous for their powerful wrestlers?

2 Where is the Gulf of Carpentaria?

3 *Snakes and Ladders* is part of the autobiography of whom?

4 In what month is the Lord Mayor's procession and show held in London?

5 Where did Jesus turn water into wine at a marriage?

ROUND 2

1 What does a phillumenist collect?

2 The most powerful man in the Chinese Communist Party died in 1997. Who was he?

Team 2

1 The Watussi or Tutsi tribe come from Burundi in Africa. What is this tribe remarkable for?

2 What is the name of the strait which separates North Island and South Island, New Zealand?

3 Whose autobiographical books include *Confessions of a Hooker, My Life-long Love Affair with Golf*?

4 When is St George's Day?

5 What bird did Noah first release after the rain abated?

1 Which word describes all these animals: voles, mice, rats and hamsters?

2 Which ex-Tory minister became 'Fat Pang' during his time in the Far East?

3 Which actress said, 'It is better to be looked over than overlooked'?

4 On what day of the week was the Grand National run in 1997?

5 What type of creature is a mugger?

ROUND 3

1 What was the name of Don Quixote's squire?

2 What are the 'northern lights' also known as?

3 Which Italian artist was responsible for a famous series of anatomical sketches?

4 On which part of the body would you have a tracheotomy?

5 What name is given to a sugar syrup gently heated until it browns?

ROUND 4

1 From which type of aircraft were the Hiroshima and Nagasaki atom bombs dropped?

2 What does *mein kampf* mean in English?

3 Who wrote the musical composition 'La Mer'?

3 Which actress wrote the book *You Can Get There From Here*?

4 Which horse won the 1998 Epsom Derby?

5 What type of insect is a devil's coach-horse?

1 What did Don Quixote mistake for evil giants?

2 Name two planets that are much bigger than the earth.

3 The artist Stubbs was most famous for painting which subjects?

4 What are Ishihara tests used for?

5 Name the highly-flavoured East Indian soup made with curry powder and hot seasoning.

1 Which company built the Vimy and the Wellington?

2 What is the actual meaning of *cosa nostra*?

3 Who composed 'Brigg Fair'?

4 What is the monetary unit of Argentina?

5 In which country would you find the volcano Villarica?

4 What is the monetary unit of Malta?

5 In which mountain range would you find the extinct volcano, Elbrus?

ROUND 5   *Individual questions for team 1*

Soccer
Which station on the Piccadilly Line is the only one in Britain named after a football club?

Famous women
Who is both chief-commandant for women in the Royal Navy and colonel-in-chief of the Royal Scots Regiment?

Name the year
In what year was the Panama Canal opened?

Nature
Which wild plant is associated with St Patrick's Day?

Spelling
Spell a word beginning with 'p' meaning *nom-de-plume*.

Team 2

Team 1

ROUND 6

1 Who is the patron saint of Venice?

2 What is a sheep ked?

3 Which Spanish monarchs financed Christopher Columbus's first voyage to the New World?

4 What is the collective noun for a group of chickens?

5 What is the capital of Sudan?

1 Which saint is the patron of travellers?

2 What is a lousewort?

3 Name the European country in which the Cortes is the parliament.

4 What is the collective noun for a group of angels?

5 What is the capital of Albania?

ROUND 7

1 What does ANZAC stand for?

2 In which Jane Austen novel did Sir Thomas Bertram and Mrs Norris appear?

3 'Ring of Fire' and 'Jackson' were hits for which country singer?

4 Which Cornish castle is associated with Arthurian legend?

5 Which TV sit-com was based in Grace Brothers store?

1 What does ERNIE stand for?

2 In Charlotte Bronte's *Jane Eyre* who does the heroine eventually marry?

3 'We All Stand Together' was a hit for which pop artist?

4 Which mythical hero is sometimes said to be buried in Glastonbury?

5 Which TV sit-com featured the Boswells?

ROUND 8

1 Name the notch in the Appalachian Mountains near the juncture of Virginia, Tennessee, and Kentucky.

2 Who succeeded Lenin after his death in 1924?

3 What is a kaftan?

4 In which country would you hear the Frisian language?

5 What did Sir Rowland Hill introduce in Britain in 1840?

1 Which rock needle overlooks Chamonix in the Mont Blanc massif?

2 What was Adolf Hitler's original family name, parodied by his opponents during and after his rise to power?

3 What is a puttee?

4 What language is spoken in Roussillon, Andorra, north-eastern Spain and the Balearic Isles?

5 Of what in sport were mufflers, invented by Jack Broughton in the second half of the eighteenth century, the forerunner?

ROUND 9

1 Which American city was almost destroyed by fire in 1871?

2 Who was MP for Peckham and in 1997 became a minister in the Labour government?

3 Who composed the music for the ballet *The Sleeping Beauty*?

4 What does MG stand for, as in the MG motor car?

5 What does NASA stand for?

1 Of which US state is Salem the capital?

2 Who lives at Nelson Mandela House, Peckham?

3 'Children's Corner' is a suite of piano pieces by which composer?

4 Which instrument measures RPM in a motor car?

5 What does ESA stand for?

ROUND 10   *Individual questions for team 2*

Soccer
Which manager guided Arsenal to the double in 1971?

Famous women
Who was a successful motor racing driver before inheriting the Windmill Theatre, which she was forced to close in 1964?

Name the year
In what year did Sir Francis Chichester win the first single-handed transatlantic yacht race?

Nature
'Pink Pearl', 'Pink Drift' and 'Pink Perfection' are hybrids of which flowering shrub?

Spelling
Spell a word beginning with 'p' which means inflammation of the throat.

Team 1 _____   *Team 2* _____

DRINKS ROUND

1 What is a person who draws up maps called?

1 What is a person who studies bird life called?

2 Which stretch of water separates Tasmania from Australia?

3 Which French artist is recognised as the co-founder of cubism?

4 Where in the USA do the football team the Cowboys come from?

5 In Spain whiteness of the skin used to be seen as a sign of nobility. What well-known expression did this give rise to?

6 In 1519 *Trinidad, San Antonio, Concepcion, Vittoria* and *Santiago* made up the fleet of which explorer?

7 Which actress starred in *The Millionairess* and *The Cassandra Crossing*?

8 Name the IRA hunger striker who died in May 1981 after 66 days' fasting.

9 What is the feminine of testator?

10 In what art form has Henri Cartier-Bresson achieved fame?

2 Where is the Bowery?

3 With which London district are the painters Walter Sickert and Frederick Spencer Gore associated?

4 Where in the USA do the football team the Dolphins come from?

5 Name the supposed city of gold which inspired the Spanish conquest of South and Central America.

6 In which war was the Battle of Inkerman fought?

7 Who was the female star of the film *Soldier Blue*?

8 Name the police constable who was awarded the George Medal for his part in the Iranian embassy siege of 1980.

9 What is the feminine of ogre?

10 Which photographer's books include *The Most Beautiful Women*?

RESERVE QUESTIONS

1 What single word describes a leg of mutton?

2 What type of fruit is a queening?

3 In which of Shakespeare's plays does Polonius appear?

15

Pub League Quiz 2

The individual questions are in Rounds 5 and 10 and are on the following subjects: Books, Also known as, Characters, Time and Pot luck.

Team 1

ROUND 1
1 What was the circus name of Nikolai Poliakov?
2 What is Paddington Bear's favourite snack?
3 What was the name of Jacques Cousteau's famous research ship?
4 On what colour square does the white king start a chess game?
5 What does FAO stand for?

ROUND 2
1 Whose story was portrayed in *The Naked Civil Servant*?
2 In which Arab country did Idi Amin take refuge in 1979?
3 What sort of young fish is a smolt?
4 What in Germany is the *Brockhaus*?

Team 2

1 Which violin-playing comedian was born Benjamin Kubelsky?
2 Which fairy story was turned into the film *The Slipper and the Rose*?
3 Name the great warship which sank off Portsmouth in 1545.
4 What is the British game of noughts and crosses called in America?
5 Where does the FAO have its headquarters?

1 Which *Peyton Place* star married Frank Sinatra?
2 Whose flight from Tibet made headlines in 1959?
3 What is a carabao?
4 What book was published for the first time in Edinburgh in 1768?

5 Which unit of currency is used in Iraq, Jordan and Tunisia?

ROUND 3

1 Who won an Oscar for playing a mentally handicapped pianist?

2 What did a Sybil utter in ancient Greece?

3 Who wrote *Little Women*?

4 How many moons has Mercury?

5 From which flower is saffron obtained?

ROUND 4

1 Which is the largest of the lakes in the United States of America?

2 In which film did Rod Steiger play the part of Police Chief Bill Gillespie?

5 Where did the pirates' 'pieces of eight' come from?

1 For her part in the film version of what play did Vivien Leigh win an Oscar in 1951?

2 What does the Bible call 'the beginning of wisdom'?

3 In which of Hardy's novels is Bathsheba Everdene the central character?

4 Which planet has two dwarf satellites called Phobos and Deimos?

5 Tied together, what do a sprig of parsley, thyme and a bay leaf comprise?

1 Which American city has the second largest number of ethnic Poles in the world after Warsaw?

2 Which 1930 film made Edward G. Robinson a star and featured the line, 'Is this the end of Rico?'

3 Which country did the Allies invade in Operation Avalanche of World War 2?

4 In which of his plays did Shakespeare write one scene entirely in French?

5 What was the *Magnus Portus* of Roman Britain?

3 What was the name given to Hitler's *Blitzkrieg* offensive against the USSR in June 1941?

4 In which city did Shakespeare set the greater part of *Romeo and Juliet*?

5 What northern town in Britain was called *Aquae* by the Romans?

ROUND 5 *Individual questions for team 1*

Books
Who created the stories of the detective called Maigret?

Also known as
What was the secret identity of Don Diego, the masked avenger?

Characters
Who was Lancelot's son in Arthurian legend?

Time
In which century was the first watch invented?

Pot luck
With which African river was Mungo Park most closely associated?

Team 2	*Team 1*

ROUND 6

1 In which sport was Irina Rodnina a world champion?

2 Where would you step out to see the Giant's Causeway?

1 In which sport was Sonja Henie a world champion?

2 In which British city is the Royal Liver Building?

3   What did Queen Victoria specifically ban from her funeral?

4   What is the largest species of shark?

5   What was the first 'garden city' in Britain, begun in 1903?

ROUND 7

1   Which gas is represented by the chemical formula CO?

2   What were featheries, gutties and putties?

3   What type of creatures appear last in the fossil record?

4   Which fruit is impossible to eat, according to a Trini Lopez song?

5   Which Scottish hero travelled under the name of Betty Burke?

ROUND 8

1   Who created Prince Caspian and Aslan?

2   What is the French word for a dowry?

3   Which subsequent head of state was born a member of the royal family of the Tembu tribe in the Transkei?

4   Name both creatures of which there is a long-eared variety.

5   What building used to be the headquarters of the commander-in-chief of the British Army?

1   What is the chemical symbol for neon?

2   Which sport uses granites?

3   How many ice ages were there in the Pliocene era?

4   Where did Ralph McTell offer to 'take you by the hand and lead you'?

5   Which country numbers William Tell among its national heroes?

1   Which novel by Grace Metalious, her first, was on the bestseller list for two years?

2   What is the word from French for a royal state reception attended only by males?

3 Which Swiss winter sports resort is the home of the Cresta Run?

4 What does the river Seine empty into?

5 Which operatic heroine commits suicide on her father's sword?

3 From which language did English adopt the word ski?

4 Which maritime country has the shortest coastline?

5 Which Mozart opera has associations with freemasonry?

ROUND 9

1 Who created the private detective Philip Marlowe?

2 Which sea-bird has the greatest wing span?

3 For which Spanish football club did Puskas and Di Stefano play?

4 For which British king did Handel compose the *Water Music*, it is said as a peace offering?

5 Who was Nikos Kazantzakis's most famous character?

1 Who took over from Roger Moore as the Saint?

2 How many front toes does a parrot have?

3 Which footballer scored a hat trick in the World Cup Final match in 1966?

4 Which English composer was most closely associated with the Aldeburgh Festival?

5 Who is credited with writing the first detective story, *The Murders in the Rue Morgue*?

ROUND 10 *Individual questions for team 2*

Books
Who wrote the book on which the film *Camille* was based?
Also known as
Who is British actor Maurice Micklewhite better known as?
Characters
What kind of school did Pussy Galore run?

Time
Who introduced leap year?
Pot luck
What was the last port of call of the *Mayflower* before setting sail for America?

Team 1	Team 2

DRINKS ROUND

1 What nationality was the painter Diego Rivera?

1 What nationality by birth was René Magritte?

2 What sea separates West and East Malaysia?

2 What large island lies east of Africa and west of Australia?

3 On the life of which religious Scottish athlete was the film *Chariots of Fire* based?

3 Which British film grossed over £50 million in the UK alone from 1997 onwards?

4 'London. Michaelmas term lately over, and the Lord Chancellor sitting in Lincoln's Inn Hall.' These are the opening lines of which novel by Dickens?

4 Which classic novel opens with the dictum, 'Every man in possession of a fortune, must be in want of a wife'?

5 In which Hitchcock film did Shirley MacLaine make her debut?

5 Which Hollywood producer said, 'A wide screen makes a bad film twice as bad'?

6 Which lord went missing when his luck ran out in 1974?

6 Who went for a swim in Miami and later emerged in Australia with two new names?

7 What precedes, 'And never the twain shall meet'?

7 Which cartoonist said, 'A woman's place is in the wrong'?

21

8 How many pairs of chromosomes does a normal person have?

9 Who succeeded Uwe Seeler as Germany's soccer captain?

10 Which South American country's name means Little Venice?

8 How often are brain cells replaced?

9 Who captained the Dutch soccer side in the 1974 World Cup?

10 Name the highest waterfall in South America.

RESERVE QUESTIONS

1 Who was the first black performer to have a Number 1 hit in the UK with 'Let's Have Another Party'?

2 What was the name of the first sheep to be cloned in Britain?

3 What does hell have no fury like?

Pub League Quiz 3

The individual questions are in Rounds 5 and 10 and are on the following subjects: Pop music, Astronomy, Drink, Motor sports and Land animals.

Team 1

ROUND 1
1 Name the author of *War and Remembrance*.
2 What is the date of Scotland's national day?
3 In which novel does the ship *Pequod* appear?
4 What was Thomas Crapper's claim to fame?
5 What in chess was 'Deep Blue'?

ROUND 2
1 Which Australian city was named after the father of the theory of evolution?
2 Which 1953 Broadway musical introduced the song 'Stranger in Paradise'?
3 What did the Tories give Tony Blair during the 1997 general election campaign to which the Advertising Standards Authority objected?

Team 2

ROUND 1
1 Name the author of *The Thorn Birds*.
2 When is St Patrick's Day?
3 Which Shakespeare play has the alternative title '*What You Will*'?
4 Under which tree is the Buddha supposed to have sat when he attained enlightenment?
5 What is a natatorium?

ROUND 2
1 What was David Livingstone's calling when he began his travels in Africa?
2 Which successful film featured the Number 1 hit 'Love Is All Around'?
3 By what name is the Parliamentary Commissioner for Administration better known?

4 Who founded the Habitat design empire?

5 Which motorway links Coventry and Leicester?

4 What kind of things did Capability Brown design?

5 Which Italian city is referred to by the 'T' in FIAT?

ROUND 3

1 Who, when asked what his golf handicap was, replied, 'I'm a one-eyed Jewish negro'?

2 Who was the first Roman Catholic president of the USA?

3 What kind of animal was Pinocchio's pet Figaro?

4 Which ship of 1906 held the Blue Riband for 22 years?

5 *Manque* and *passe* are terms in what game?

1 Which comedian quipped, 'President Johnson says a war isn't really a war without my jokes'?

2 After which American president is the capital of Liberia named?

3 What do Tiggers do best?

4 Which liner was the last holder of the Atlantic Blue Riband?

5 How many back-gammon pieces does each player start with?

ROUND 4

1 What is the name of the TV Addams family's butler?

2 How many strings has a cello?

3 Which European city has become famous for its gnomes?

4 Who wrote *Round the Bend*?

1 In which country was the TV series *Crane* set?

2 In music what word means to displace beats or accents so that what was 'strong' becomes 'weak', and vice versa?

3 In which American state is Fort Knox?

4 Who wrote the poem 'The Rolling English Road'?

5 Which composer said of another, 'Wagner has lovely moments but awful quarters of an hour'?

5 Who called religion 'the opium of the people'?

ROUND 5 *Individual questions for team 1*

Pop music
Who sang 'Silver Lady'?

Astronomy
What is the disc or halo round the sun called?

Drink
What is known as the 'queen' among drinks?

Motor sports
Who won the 1962 Grand Prix world championship in a BRM?

Land animals
Which venomous serpent is also known as the pit viper?

Team 2	*Team 1*

ROUND 6

1 What do Ryan Giggs, Richard Burton and Augustus John have in common?

1 In which country does a true Bohemian live?

2 Who, by the age of 13, had composed concertos, symphonies, sonatas and operettas?

2 Which composer was the subject of the film *The Music Lovers*?

3 What was erected overnight in August 1961?

3 Something special happened to the Archbishop of Cracow in 1978. What was it?

4 Who created Harry Lime?

4 Who was Dorothy L. Sayers' aristocratic sleuth?

5 Which bird lays the largest eggs?

5 Which bird lays the largest eggs in proportion to its size?

ROUND 7

1 What are the initials of the governing body of world soccer?

1 After whom was the soccer World Cup trophy named?

2 Where did the first *Road To* film set off to in 1940?

2 Where was *A Bridge Too Far*?

3 Which Dustin Hoffman film took place in a Cornish village?

3 In which film was Dustin Hoffman seen approaching a swimming pool in a wetsuit?

4 Which famous speech was described in the press as 'silly, flat and dishwatery'?

4 Which composer once said, 'Competitions are for horses, not artists'?

5 Who wrote *The Trial* and *The Castle*?

5 Who wrote *Death In Venice*?

ROUND 8

1 By what name is Michael Dumble-Smith better known?

1 Who is Lesley Hornby better known as?

2 Who succeeded Stalin as USSR premier?

2 Who succeeded Lincoln as president of the USA?

3 What nationality was Aladdin?

3 What nationality was El Cid?

4 Which European capital is home to the world's most accurate mechanical clock?

4 Which English cathedral has the oldest surviving working clock in the world?

5 The waters of which ocean wash against Copacobana beach?

5 Which tropical island paradise lies 400 miles south-west of Sri Lanka?

ROUND 9

1 Who was emperor of China when Marco Polo visited his court?

2 To whom was Natalie Wood married when she died?

3 Who, with his twin Remus, was suckled by a wolf?

4 What is the study of fossils called?

5 Which is the smallest of the Great Lakes?

1 What were Baffin, Frobisher and Franklin all searching for?

2 Who was Laurence Olivier's first wife?

3 Which day of the week is named after the Norse goddess of love?

4 What branch of science is called after the Greek for 'house'?

5 Which international border is crossed the most?

ROUND 10   *Individual questions for team 2*

Pop music
Who sang 'When Will I See You Again'?
Astronomy
Which planet is farthest from the sun?
Drink
Name the blind Benedictine monk who invented the first true sparkling champagne.
Motor sports
Which world champion racing driver was born in Milton, Dunbartonshire?
Land animals
Which mammal is considered to be the tallest?

Team 1	*Team 2*

DRINKS ROUND

1 Who infuriated Mae West by calling her 'My Little Brood Mare'?

1 In which film does Groucho Marx say, 'Either this guy's dead or my watch has stopped'?

27

Q 3

2 What is a dipsomaniac?

3 For which county cricket side did W.G. Grace play?

4 Which US state capital has the most Buddhist temples?

5 What did 'Doctor Bob S.' and 'Bill W.' found in June 1935?

6 Which poet popularised the limerick?

7 What term applies to space devoid of matter?

8 What is the name of the pre-match war dance performed by the New Zealand rugby team?

9 Which Asian country has the other name of Bharat?

10 What has to be produced in a writ of *habeas corpus*?

2 Which part of the body is affected by cirrhosis?

3 Who was the first Australian cricketer to be knighted?

4 Which German directed the film *The Marriage of Maria Braun*?

5 How many pints in a gill?

6 Which American state borders only one other?

7 To what use was nitrous oxide first put in 1842?

8 Ninian Park is the home of which soccer club?

9 Which country is nicknamed 'the roof of the world'?

10 Whose law states, 'If anything can go wrong it will'?

RESERVE QUESTIONS
1 Who was King Zog?
2 What is the more usual name for the bird *Turdus merula*?
3 What type of salad ingredient is a cos?

Pub League Quiz 4

The individual questions are in Rounds 5 and 10 and are on the following subjects: TV and radio, Ships, Geography, Classical music and Kings and queens.

Team 1

ROUND 1
1 Into which sea does the river Danube flow?

2 What was the pseudonym of Henri Charrière, famous escaper?

3 What is the name of the governing body of the Roman Catholic Church?

4 In 1941 the British sank a German ship bearing the name of Germany's Iron Chancellor. What was it?

5 In which sport is *yokozuna* the rank of a grand champion?

ROUND 2
1 Which architect designed the Cenotaph in Whitehall?

Team 2

1 What country was known as the 'cockpit of Europe'?

2 What was the assumed name of François-Marie Arouet, French poet and dramatist?

3 Who is the Vicar of Christ?

4 What was the main base for British submarines during World War 2?

5 Who became world snooker champion, aged 21, in 1990?

1 Which great country house north of Leeds is the seat of the Lascelles family?

2 In the 1860s, Louis Dobermann developed a breed of dog to protect him at work. What was his profession?

3 In which book by Charles Dickens would you find Bill Sikes?

4 What is the knob at the front of a horse saddle called?

5 Who first reached the South Pole?

ROUND 3

1 What is the name of the ceremony at which a prime minister accepts the seals of office from the Queen?

2 Who played Miss Jones in *Rising Damp*?

3 Who wrote *The Lord of the Rings*?

4 What does RNLI stand for?

5 Which US president had previously commanded the invasion of North Africa (1942) and the allied invasion of Europe (1944)?

2 What is a miniature foxhound used for coursing hares called?

3 What was the actual name of the Artful Dodger?

4 *Sayonara* is 'goodbye' in which language?

5 Who found and opened Tutankhamen's tomb in 1922?

1 What is the name of the hall in New York which is the headquarters of the Democratic Party?

2 Who played Detective Sergeant Harriet Makepeace in *Dempsey and Makepeace*?

3 Who wrote *Wuthering Heights*?

4 What does NATO stand for?

5 Who was the USSR premier at the time of the Cuban missile crisis?

ROUND 4

1 Where would you find the Trevi Fountain?

2 Within five years, when was the BBC established?

3 Which royal personage said of another royal personage, 'After I am dead the boy will ruin himself in 12 months'?

4 Which rank is below a colonel and above a major in the British Army?

5 Whose book of poems *Les Fleurs du Mal* was declared obscene in 1857?

1 In which present-day country is the ancient city of Ephesus?

2 Within five years, when was the first *Radio Times* published?

3 What does the third quarter, 'azure, a harp or stringed argent', represent on the Royal Arms?

4 Which rank is below a group captain and above a squadron leader in the Royal Air Force?

5 Who was Jean-Baptiste Poquelin better known as?

Q 4

ROUND 5 *Individual questions for team 1*

TV and radio
Name the radio doctor who became chairman of the Independent Television Authority and then chairman of the governors of the BBC.

Ships
What was the name of the world's first atomic-powered merchant ship launched in 1959?

Geography
Which is the southernmost state of the USA?

Classical music
Name Prokofiev's orchestral piece in which a narrator tells a fairy tale.

Kings and queens
Overthrown by Alexander the Great, Darius III was king of which country?

ROUND 6

1 Who was hanged for the 'A6 murder' of 1961?

2 Which French footballer and philosopher declared, 'When the seagulls follow the trawler, it is because they think sardines will be thrown into the sea'?

3 Which species of fox is most common in Europe?

4 What is the feminine of gaffer?

5 What nationality was Alfred Sisley, the artist?

1 What other profession did publican Albert Pierrepoint follow?

2 Which French philosopher was of the opinion that 'hell is other people'?

3 Which is the largest deer native to Britain?

4 What is the feminine of votary?

5 What nationality was the painter Jackson Pollock?

ROUND 7

1 In which fictional borough is *Coronation Street*?

2 Which gulf extends along the coast of France from the Spanish border to Toulon?

3 Which famous photographer brought Jean Shrimpton to the fore as a model?

4 Who abandoned the cinema in 1938 but wrote *Lulu in Hollywood* in 1982?

1 *Casualty* is set in which thinly disguised British city?

2 Of which country are the Chatham Islands a part?

3 Which Italian designer was murdered in Miami in 1997?

4 Which top American mobster was deported by both the USA and Cuba, before finding sanctuary in Naples?

5 Which star won an Oscar for playing the title role in the film *Hamlet*?

5 Which actress won an Oscar for her part in the film *On Golden Pond*?

ROUND 8

1 Which of the four gospels is thought to be based on eye-witness information?

1 Who removed the thorn from the lion's foot?

2 Of what was Pan the god?

2 Who was the father of Pan?

3 In the placings on a cricket field, what position stands between cover point and mid off?

3 What is the home ground of Surrey County Cricket Club?

4 What was the trade of George Ravenscroft?

4 What was the trade of Peter Carl Fabergé?

5 What does *stet* mean?

5 What does FD stand for?

ROUND 9

1 On which river is the city of Chester?

1 What port is at the mouth of the Scottish Dee?

2 Who was the governor of the Bahamas during World War 2?

2 Which British prime minister worked as a research chemist in industry?

3 Where in the USA are there four busts of presidents carved on the face of a mountain?

3 Name the four presidents carved on Mount Rushmore.

4 Which character in *Red Dwarf* is preoccupied with fashion?

4 Which character in *Red Dwarf* is a hologram?

5 What was the venue for the 1948 Olympics and for the Live Aid concert of 1985?

5 What great sporting event took place at Squaw Valley in 1985?

ROUND 10 *Individual questions for team 2*

TV and radio
Why are soap operas so called?
Ships
Which German battleship was outmanoeuvered by three British cruisers and finally scuttled in the river Plate in 1939?
Geography
Which kingdom of North Africa has a Mediterranean coastline?
Classical music
Who composed the opera *La Clemenza di Tito*?
Kings and queens
Which country did Casimir III rule over?

Team 1	Team 2

DRINKS ROUND

1 Who played the male lead in the film *The Graduate*?

1 What part did Anne Bancroft play in *The Graduate*?

2 What is a gaur?

2 What is a wheatear?

3 Name the three Cromwells who played a prominent part in English religious and political life in the sixteenth and seventeenth centuries.

3 What religious office did the Benedictine Lanfranc hold in England from 1070 to 1089?

4 Who is the highest legal ranking officer in England and Wales?

4 Who is the second highest legal ranking officer in England and Wales?

5 Who wrote the novel *Hard Times*?

5 Who wrote *The Naked and the Dead*?

6 Where are the Lofoten Islands?

6 What is the second largest city in Poland?

7 Which singer was christened Annie Mae Bullock?

8 Which number doubled, exceeds its half by nine?

9 What penal system for young offenders was named after a village near Rochester in Kent?

10 What colour is the gemstone lapis lazuli?

7 Which rock artist was christened William Perks?

8 Two numbers add up to 19. One is twice the other plus one. What are they?

9 What was the real name of the 'Boston Strangler'?

10 What is another word for plumbago or black-lead?

RESERVE QUESTIONS

1 Which dog is the main character of the *Peanuts* cartoon?

2 In which activity might you perform a 'Bob Major' or 'Grandsire Triple'?

3 Who died instantly when she saw Sir Lancelot on horseback?

Pub League Quiz 5

The individual questions are in Rounds 5 and 10 and are on the following subjects: History and warfare, Law, Pot luck, Literature and Words.

Team 1

ROUND 1

1 What name is usually given to the wild rose of the English countryside?

2 The shanny is the most common British species of what sort of fish?

3 Who in religion was born in Mecca?

4 Name the famous mausoleum at Agra.

5 Where was home to Yogi Bear?

ROUND 2

1 Who starred with Jeanette Macdonald in the 1940 film musical *Bitter Sweet*?

2 Which Italian poet was famous for the *Divine Comedy*?

3 Which great waterway opened on 16 November 1869?

4 In mythology, which youth fell in love with his own reflection?

Team 2

1 What sort of fruits are Ashton Crosses, Bedford Giants and Fantasies?

2 Which arborial marsupial feeds off eucalyptus leaves?

3 In which city is the tomb of Mohammed?

4 In which city is Carnegie Hall?

5 Which cartoonist created Bogart, the cat?

1 Which American actress starred in the films *Jezebel* and *All About Eve*?

2 Who wrote the series of poems *Idylls of the King*?

3 Which waterway links Loch Linnhie with the Moray Firth?

4 Who in mythology were supposed to have hatched from an egg?

5 Who is fourth in line of succession to the British throne?

5 What relation is the Duke of Kent to HM the Queen?

ROUND 3

1 Name the branch of medicine which deals with childbirth, ante-natal and post-natal care.

1 What is the study of family origins and descendants called?

2 Where are the Diamond Sculls competed for?

2 What is the country of origin of *taekwondo*?

3 Who wrote the opera *The Magic Flute*?

3 Who wrote the opera *The Barber of Seville*?

4 Who discovered penicillin?

4 Who introduced mercury thermometers?

5 What does BChD stand for?

5 What does BCL stand for?

ROUND 4

1 Who played Alf Garnett's son-in-law in *Till Death Us Do Part*?

1 Which actress played Alf Garnett's wife in *Till Death Us Do Part*?

2 From what are marshmallows prepared?

2 What sort of plant blooms every two years?

3 What would you find at the parallel of latitude 23.5° north of the equator?

3 What connects the Kabul river with Peshawar in Pakistan?

4 Who created Brer Rabbit?

4 Who wrote *The Return of the Native*?

5 Who assassinated Abraham Lincoln?

5 To whom did General Robert E. Lee surrender in the American Civil War?

ROUND 5   *Individual questions for team 1*

History and warfare
Where was the so-called 'Battle of the Nations' in 1813?
Law
What in law is easement?
Pot luck
What was a Lee-Enfield?
Literature
Which playwright, author of *Tamburlaine the Great*, was killed in a tavern brawl?
Words
Which word means an assembly of witches?

Team 2	Team 1

ROUND 6

Team 2

1 What unit weighs 200 milligrams?
2 Which boxer was nick-named the 'Brown Bomber'?
3 Who is on public record as saying of the presentation of debutantes at court, 'We had to stop them. Every tart in London was being presented'?
4 In which English county is Sleap aerodrome?
5 In which parish is Dawn French a TV vicar?

Team 1

1 What is equivalent to 1,852 metres?
2 Who was Pearl White?
3 Which statesman is supposed to have said, 'This is the sort of English up with which I will not put'?
4 What is the most southerly point of England?
5 In which series of television comedies does Baldrick appear?

ROUND 7

1 Who wrote *Sword Blades and Poppy Seed*?
2 What is a pangolin?
3 Where was the first Test Match in England held?
4 What has been located at Llantrisant, Wales, since 1968?
5 What is the second city and chief port of the Netherlands?

1 Who wrote *The Four Zoas*?
2 What is a merganser?
3 In which country did Grand Prix racing begin?
4 What was the trade of Thomas Minton, who died in 1836?
5 Which two rivers meet at Duisburg, one of the largest inland ports in Europe?

Q
5

ROUND 8

1 Name two of the nine Muses in Greek mythology.
2 Within ten years, when was the first game of rugby played?
3 Which English king was nicknamed Rufus?
4 What in pottery is biscuitware?
5 What date was the siege of Ladysmith (months and years)?

1 Name four of the Muses' arts.
2 Within ten years, when was the Rugby Union formed?
3 Which English king was nicknamed Lionheart?
4 What is celadon glaze?
5 What date was the siege of La Rochelle (years)?

ROUND 9

1 Who wrote, 'The Holy Roman Empire was neither holy, nor Roman, nor an empire'?
2 What does hepatitis infect?

1 Who said, 'No man but a blockhead ever wrote, except for money'?
2 What does gingivitis infect?

3 Julius Caesar had a son called Caesarion. Who was his mother?

4 Where is Nelson buried?

5 In which film did Charlie Chaplin first speak?

3 Who was the husband of Roxana?

4 Where was Thomas à Becket murdered?

5 In which film did Ronald Reagan appear as General George Custer?

ROUND 10 *Individual questions for team 2*

History and warfare

A meeting took place between Churchill, Stalin and Roosevelt during World War 2 to decide the fate of Europe after the fall of Hitler's Germany. Where was this held?

Law

What were the criminal courts held four times a year by legal justices of the peace in England and Wales called?

Pot luck

The Jewish patriarch Abraham was born at Ur of the Chaldees. In which modern country is Ur?

Literature

Who according to Shakespeare in *King Lear* is 'the prince of darkness'?

Words

What name is given to the study or collection of coins, tokens and medals?

Team 1

Team 2

DRINKS ROUND

1 Whom did Ffion Jenkins marry in 1997?

2 What year was Earl Mountbatten murdered by the IRA?

1 Who married Brooke Shields in 1997?

2 Who was vice-president of the USA in 1978?

3 Who in the seventeenth century wrote the dictum which translates to English as, 'The heart has its reasons which reason knows nothing of'?

4 What was the metal frame called that women used to wear to make their dresses stand out?

5 What is the capital of Minorca?

6 Who wrote *Separate Tables*?

7 What was the composer Bizet's Christian name?

8 What does HMSO stand for?

9 What is an egret?

10 What is either a red precious stone or a skin infection worse than a boil?

3 Who in 1558 published a pamphlet entitled 'The First Blast of the Trumpet Against the Monstrous Regiment of Women'?

4 What is the Scottish woollen cap with a crease down the crown called?

Q
5

5 Of which country is Mogadishu the capital?

6 Who wrote *Murder in the Cathedral*?

7 What was the Swiss composer Honegger's given name?

8 What does ASLEF stand for?

9 What is a teal?

10 Where in your body are both your alveoli and pleura?

RESERVE QUESTIONS

1 Why is the Trinity site, near Alamogordo, New Mexico, historically important?

2 Which cocktail is made of gin, Cointreau and lemon juice?

3 How should a series of notes be played that are marked 'staccato'?

Pub League Quiz 6

The individual questions are in Rounds 5 and 10 and are on the following subjects: History, Entertainment, Animals, Literature and Aircraft.

Team 1

Team 2

ROUND 1

1 Where is the highest airport in the world?

2 The Ligurian Sea indents the north-western coast of which country?

3 Which cathedral has a steeple known as 'Old Steve'?

4 Which king died after being thrown against his horse's pommel?

5 How old was Joan of Arc when she was burnt at the stake?

1 What do the initials QANTAS represent?

2 Where is the Massabielle grotto?

3 Name the cathedral in Venice.

4 In what language did King George I and his ministers converse?

5 How old was the Emperor Nero when he committed suicide?

ROUND 2

1 In which town did the Wars of the Roses begin?

2 How did Billy Connolly spell his Number 1 UK hit of 1975?

3 The plays *Dear Brutus* and *Mary Rose* were written by whom?

1 Which moor was the scene of a decisive battle in the English Civil War on 2 July 1644?

2 Who recorded 'Y.M.C.A.' in 1978?

3 What is J.M. Barrie's most famous work?

4 Who composed *Die Fledermaus?*

4 What is the English translation of *Die Fledermaus?*

5 Which word means a place for sporting activity in England but a school of the highest grade in Germany?

5 Modern pentathlon consists of cross-country riding and running, epée fencing, swimming and which other sport?

ROUND 3

1 What does IBM stand for?

1 What does IMF stand for?

2 Name the two British hostages incarcerated with Terry Waite in Beirut before being finally released in August 1991.

2 Which great composer's first musical experience came when he was appointed bandmaster for the staff of a lunatic asylum?

3 What is the libretto of an opera?

3 When is an opera a grand opera?

4 What nationality was Rubens?

4 What nationality was Whistler?

5 Whose victims were Mary Nichols, Elizabeth Stride, Catharine Eddowes, Mary Kelly and Eliza Chapman?

5 What London address is infamous for the crimes of John Christie and Timothy Evans?

ROUND 4

1 Which religious body was founded by George Fox in the seventeenth century?

1 What name is given to the Japanese school of Buddhism?

2 Who played Lawrence of Arabia in the film of the same name?

2 Which actor won an Oscar for his role in *One Flew Over the Cuckoo's Nest?*

3 Where are the Aberdare range of mountains?

3 Where is the volcano Mauna Loa?

Q
6

4 What is the name given to a solution of opium in alcohol that used to be given as a tranquilliser?

5 Where were the Nazi war crimes trials, 1945–46 held?

4 What drug derived from the peyote cactus of Texas and northern Mexico was a forerunner of LSD?

5 Which embroidery depicts the Norman conquest of England?

ROUND 5 *Individual questions for team 1*

History
Who was the first king of the House of Windsor?

Entertainment
On which Shakespeare play is the 1938 musical *The Boys from Syracuse* based?

Animals
What sort of creature is a dragonet?

Literature
What is the more usual name for the ancient Egyptian *Book of Coming Forth by Day*?

Aircraft
The earliest jet engine to be run on test, in April 1937, was designed by whom?

Team 2   *Team 1*

ROUND 6

1 In tennis what is the women's equivalent of the Davis Cup?

1 The Preakness and Belmont Stakes are two of the three legs of the American Triple Crown for thoroughbreds. What is the third?

2 Which city was known in Roman times as Byzantium?

2 Which city was known in Roman times as Mediolanum?

3 Name four of Henry VIII's wives.

3 Name one more of his wives.

4 What is the plural of genus?

5 How did a clepsydra measure time?

4 What is the plural of genesis?

5 What is an Archimedes screw used for?

ROUND 7

1 Who had a hit with 'The Carnival is Over', in 1965?

2 In military terms, what does RHA stand for?

3 Which soccer club plays at Highfield Road?

4 What does the 'W' stand for in F.W. Woolworth?

5 Who painted a tin of Campbell's soup?

1 Who had a hit with 'It's Now or Never' in 1960?

2 In military terms, what does REME stand for?

3 Which soccer club plays at Deepdale Road?

4 Name the first large department store to open in Britain.

5 Who was the girl in Peter Sellers' soup, in the film?

ROUND 8

1 What is a bean weevil?

1 Which insect makes a ticking sound and tunnels through wood, especially in old buildings?

2 Who wrote the novel *The Four Just Men* and the play *The Squeaker*?

3 Which river flows through the capital of Afghanistan?

4 Who caused the Trojan War by abducting Helen?

5 What is removed in a meniscectomy?

2 Who wrote the novel *Mary Barton* and a life of Charlotte Bronte?

3 In which African country is the city Kananga?

4 To house which creature was the labyrinth in Crete built?

5 What would be removed in a mastectomy?

Q 6

ROUND 9

1 What did John Peake Knight invent which were used unsuccessfully in 1866, and then not again for over half a century?

2 Which two actors teamed up in *The Streets of San Francisco* on TV?

3 Which famous clergyman 'had a dream'?

4 What is the main spice used in Hungarian goulash?

5 Who composed the music for the French national anthem?

1 Who invented dynamite?

2 What was the name of the leading character in *Hawaii Five-O*?

3 Which country violated the Locarno Pact in 1936?

4 From what is the spice mace obtained?

5 The words of which country's national anthem are the oldest?

ROUND 10 *Individual questions for team 2*

History
What nationality was the prince known as Henry the Navigator?
Entertainment
Name the two stars of the film *Midnight Cowboy*.
Animals
Which is the largest British wild bird?
Literature
Name one of the volumes comprising J.R.R. Tolkein's *Lord of the Rings*.
Aircraft
To the nearest Mach number, how fast does Concorde cruise?

Team 1	Team 2

DRINKS ROUND

Team 1

1 In which of Sheridan's plays do Sir Lucius O'Trigger and Sir Anthony Absolute appear?

2 Who played the title role in the 1964 film *Seven Faces of Dr Lao*?

3 What do Mackenzie, Nelson, Peace and Churchill have in common?

4 Which American actress announced in 1998 that she had become pregnant by artificial insemination from a secret donor?

5 What is the 'city' in the Bay City Rollers?

6 Which is Britain's smallest national park?

7 Name the two stars of TV's *Never The Twain*.

8 Who became editor of *Woman* in 1893 and later wrote successful novels about Burslem and district?

9 What name used to be given to an East Indian seaman, derived from the Persian for 'army' or 'camp'?

Team 2

1 Which poet of Huguenot descent wrote *Songs of Childhood* under the pseudonym Walter Ramal?

2 Which actor became a star in the 1931 film *The Public Enemy*?

3 What did Flamsteed, Bradley, Bliss, Halley and Maskelyne have in common?

4 Who starred in the film of *Bad Timing* and later married its director, Nicholas Roeg?

5 What was Sting's profession before he took to singing?

6 Which is Britian's largest national park?

7 Which TV show featured the Campbells and the Tates?

8 What was the nickname of Australian aviator Donald Bennett?

9 Who would you be likely to see using water for 'panning'?

Q
6

| 10 What name is given to teeth used for grinding? | 10 What name is given to teeth used for tearing? |

RESERVE QUESTIONS

1 What is the Greek word for 'the anointed one' of Judaism?
2 To whom was James Boswell biographer?
3 What word describes a social system in which a woman is the wife of several men simultaneously?

Q
6

Pub League Quiz 7

The individual questions are in Rounds 5 and 10 and are on the following subjects: Pop music, Children's books, Classical music, Pot luck and History.

Team 1

ROUND 1

1 Who played Benny Hawkins in *Crossroads*?

2 What sporting event has taken place at Sebring, Riverside, Watkins Glen and Phoenix?

3 What is the square root of a million?

4 Within 50 years, when did Edward, the Black Prince, die?

5 A true cockney is born within the sound of which bells?

ROUND 2

1 Which two countries occupy the Scandinavian peninsula?

2 What is a *berceuse*?

3 What is a stockmarket share price called that is halfway between that at which a dealer will sell and at which he/she will buy?

Team 2

ROUND 1

1 In which fictional village was the Crossroads motel?

2 What 'major' event is played on the Augusta National course?

3 What is the square root of a gross?

4 Where is the ruby known as the 'Black Prince Ruby' to be found today?

5 In which thoroughfare is St Mary-le-Bow?

ROUND 2

1 What is the capital of Norway?

2 What is an *ayah*?

3 In mercantile matters, the price of an article may be quoted as inclusive of c.i.f. What do these letters stand for?

4 'The Visit to the Quack Doctor' is a part of what series of paintings by Hogarth?

5 In the West, what date is Michaelmas?

ROUND 3

1 Where in London can you find the Monument?

2 Who wrote *Paradise Lost*?

3 Who played Sue Ellen in *Dallas*?

4 Milk of magnesia is a suspension in water of which chemical?

5 What is a marsupial?

ROUND 4

1 To where did the prophet Mohammed and his followers flee in 622?

2 What was Burt Lancaster's profession before he became an actor?

3 Whose autobiography was called *Upwardly Mobile*?

4 Which Pacific island is famous for its curious hieroglyphs and formidable stone-carved statues?

4 Which artist was born in Malaga in 1881 and died at Mougins in 1973?

5 What is celebrated at Michaelmas?

1 Why was the Monument built?

2 What was the sequel to *Paradise Lost*?

3 Who played Bobby in *Dallas*?

4 Which group of drugs is called 'uppers'?

5 Which present-day animal most resembles the mastodon?

1 What name is given to the person who calls Muslims to prayer?

2 In which film did Peter Fonda and Dennis Hopper star as motor-cyclists?

3 Which British institution's motto is 'In Utmost Good Faith'?

4 Under whose jurisdiction does Norfolk Island come?

Q 7

5 What are Wyandotte, Buff Orpington and Rhode Island Red?

5 What are Romney Marsh, Suffolk, Clun Forest and Swaledale?

ROUND 5   *Individual questions for team 1*

Pop music
Name the one British member of the American group The Monkees.

Children's books
Who began a famous book, 'One thing is certain, that the *white* kitten had nothing to do with it…'?

Classical music
Die Lustige Witwe is the title of an opera by which composer?

Pot luck
What is one nautical mile per hour usually called?

History
Who was the first tsar of all Russia?

Q 7

Team 2 | **Team 1**

ROUND 6

1 Whose last novel was *Resurrection*?

1 Who wrote the verse novel *Eugene Onegin*?

2 How is information received that is *sub rosa*?

2 What does the Latin *Dei gratia* mean?

3 Where in Liverpool did the Beatles perform 292 times?

3 Which pop group took their name from a school in south Manchester?

4 What does AIM stand for?

4 What is HOLMES?

5 In which country would you find the Murchison river?

5 In which country would you find the Murchison falls?

ROUND 7

1 What name is given to a word that reads the same forwards and backwards?

2 What building housed the Great Exhibition of 1851?

3 What nationality is the star of TV's *Vets in Practice*, Trude Mostue?

4 Of which country is Maputo the capital?

5 Who wrote the play *Venus Observed*?

1 What is a dimeter?

2 Who opened the Great Exhibition of 1851?

3 What is the Christian name of the Queen of Norway?

4 Of which country is Paramaribo the capital?

5 Who wrote the play *Forty Years On*?

ROUND 8

1 Who painted the frescoes in the Vatican, 'The School of Athens' and 'Disputa'?

2 In Norse mythology, where did slain heroes go?

3 Which football team plays at Somerton Road?

4 What was the name of the butler in *Upstairs, Downstairs*?

5 What does FRSA stand for?

1 Who painted frescoes showing scenes from Genesis, on the ceiling of the Sistine Chapel?

2 In Roman mythology, who was the supreme god?

3 Which football team plays at the Hawthorns?

4 Which actress starred in *Butterflies*?

5 What does FRCM stand for?

ROUND 9

1 Which plant, often seen in rock gardens, is also known as sea-pink?

1 Which trailing purple-flowered plant, widely planted in rock gardens, is also known as purple rock-cress?

2 In which country would you find the Eucumbene dam?

2 In which American state is the Hoover dam?

3 Who wrote the novel *Of Human Bondage*?

3 Who wrote the novel *Of Mice and Men*?

4 Who followed Benjamin Disraeli as prime minister?

4 Who followed A.J. Balfour as prime minister?

5 What is the monetary unit of Panama?

5 What is the monetary unit of the Czech Republic?

Q
7

ROUND 10   *Individual questions for team 2*

Pop music
Name three of the five kinds of 'spice' originally on offer from the Spice Girls.

Children's books
In *Stalky & Co.* by Rudyard Kipling, which two boys comprise the 'Co.'?

Classical music
George II established the custom, still followed today, of the audience standing for which piece of music?

Pot luck
The stigma of a flower is the receptacle for which minute grains, essential for reproduction?

History
Name the daughter of Oedipus by his mother Jocasta.

Team 1	Team 2

DRINKS ROUND

Team 1	Team 2
1 What is represented by G in scientific texts?	**1** What is the SI unit of work and energy?
2 Name the Roman road that connects Exeter, Bath and Lincoln.	**2** Which Roman road left London by what is now the Edgware Road?
3 In which country are the Taurus mountains?	**3** What is British Honduras now called?
4 Who composed *Pictures at an Exhibition*?	**4** Who composed the music for the opera *Parsifal*?
5 Which *Coronation Street* character was shot dead in a wages snatch?	**5** In *Coronation Street*, whose first wife was killed in a car crash?
6 Who wrote *Lady Chatterley's Lover*?	**6** Who wrote *The Day of the Jackal*?
7 What does EFTA stand for?	**7** What does LNER stand for?
8 Who were known as the 'little princes in the Tower'?	**8** When Napoleon abdicated in 1814, who became king of France?
9 Who co-starred with Celia Johnson in *Brief Encounter*?	**9** Who played Solitaire in the James Bond film *Live and Let Die*?
10 Who in the nursery rhyme had 'rings on her fingers and bells on her toes'?	**10** In the nursery rhyme, who did Simple Simon meet?

RESERVE QUESTIONS

1 What, according to the proverb, does an old ox make?

2 What large, carnivorous, wolf-like marsupial became extinct in the 1930s?

3 Pertussis is which infectious disease?

Pub League Quiz 8

The individual questions are in Rounds 5 and 10 and are on the following subjects: Sport, Soap operas, England, Science and Art.

Team 1	Team 2

ROUND 1

1 Who wrote *Rebecca*?

1 Who wrote *Cannery Row*?

2 Who was responsible for *The Creation, The Seasons* and the Austrian national anthem?

2 Whose oratorios included *The Dream of Gerontius*?

3 What is the capital of Zambia?

3 Which port is the capital of Oman?

4 What is the shape of a pillar known as a caryatid?

4 What is nacre also known as?

5 What was Stewart Granger's real name?

5 What was James Stewart's real name?

ROUND 2

1 Who was the maker of the world famous Mosquito aircraft?

1 Who was the maker of the World War 2 Lightning aircraft?

2 What are *farfalle, fettuccine* and *rigatoni*?

2 Which vegetables are usually used in *ratatouille*?

3 Women in Britain were first enfranchised in 1918. How old did they have to be to vote?

3 What famous building burned down in London in 1936?

4 Joseph Priestley discovered it and called it dephlogisticated air. What do we call it now?

4 What stands between a whole gale and a hurricane on the Beaufort scale of wind force?

5 Who wrote the novels *Farewell My Lovely* and *The Long Goodbye*?

5 Who, in 1912, wrote the novel *The Lost World*?

ROUND 3

1 In TV's *Hi-De-Hi!* who played Gladys Pugh?

2 Who won five swimming gold medals, plus a silver and a bronze, at the Seoul Olympics?

3 Who wrote the line, 'A little learning is a dang'rous thing'?

4 What hit TV pro-gramme was launched on New Year's Day 1964 from a converted church hall in Manchester?

5 What word, originally the name of a fort captured by David, is a synonym for Jerusalem?

1 In *Coronation Street* who played Betty Turpin?

2 At what team sport did Britain win a gold medal at the Seoul Olympics?

3 Who said, 'A radical is a man with both feet firmly planted in the air'?

4 Elvis Presley stood on British soil only once – on 2 March 1960. Where?

5 In which modern country is the town of Tarsus where St Paul was born?

ROUND 4

1 Who is the patron saint of goldsmiths?

2 What type of creature is a cockchafer?

3 What does NFT stand for?

4 Which member of the royal family wrote a best-selling book for children entitled *The Old Man of Lochnagar*?

1 Who is the patron saint of sailors?

2 What type of creature is an anaconda?

3 What does FT stand for?

4 What is the date of HM the Queen's official birthday?

5 Who lost the French presidency to François Mitterand in 1981?

5 Which British prime minister's last words were said to be, 'Die, my dear Doctor, that's the last thing I shall do!'?

ROUND 5 *Individual questions for team 1*

Sport
Epée and foil are two forms of fencing competition. Name the third.

Soap operas
In which state was *Dynasty* set?

England
Which city did Matthew Arnold describe as 'home of lost causes and forsaken beliefs'?

Science
Which Greek scientist lost his life to a Roman soldier in Syracuse at the age of 75 in 212 BC?

Art
Which Spanish artist became court painter to Philip IV when he was only 25?

Q 8

Team 2   *Team 1*

ROUND 6

1 Which country lost to Italy in the World Cup final in 1982?

1 What type of sportsman would participate in barrel jumping?

2 Who won an Oscar for his role as an alcoholic in the 1945 film *The Lost Weekend*?

2 Which actor won Oscars in both 1937 and 1938?

3 Which South African state was known as Basutoland until 1966?

3 Zimbabwe used to be the British colony of Southern Rhodesia. What is Northern Rhodesia now called?

4 Which Canadian newspaper magnate held high government office in England during both world wars?

5 What kind of creatures are portrayed in the book *Watership Down*?

4 Which leader of the Russian revolution became Commissar for War but was expelled from the party in 1927 and assassinated in Mexico in 1940?

5 What was the name of the castaway sailor whose adventures led to Daniel Defoe writing *Robinson Crusoe*?

ROUND 7

1 What sort of creature is a laughing jackass?

2 What is a mignonette?

3 What, according to the legal saying, do hard cases make?

4 Which of the T.S. Eliot/ Lloyd Webber cats is named after a book of the Bible?

5 In which country is cricket's Sheffield Shield competed for?

1 What is an oryx?

2 What variety of plum, yellow, dark purple or blue to black, has small, oval fruit?

3 What fictional barrister is played by John Thaw?

4 What is the last book of the Bible?

5 Name two of the famous 1950 Alfa Romeo team.

ROUND 8

1 Which architect designed the layout of Regent's Park and Regent Street?

1 Which architect designed the Guggenheim museum?

2 Who was the student leader who died in police custody in South Africa in 1977?

3 Which TV quiz show is hosted by Michael Barrymore?

4 Who wrote the comedy *The Government Inspector*?

5 What famous university is located at Ithaca, New York?

ROUND 9

1 Which Wimbledon champion married and was then known as Mrs Court?

2 What was Nelson's rank at Trafalgar?

3 In which city did the assassination of Martin Luther King take place?

4 Where in Scotland is Queen Street railway station?

5 Which American film-maker made many epics on biblical themes including *Samson and Delilah* and *The Ten Commandments*?

2 Which film by Richard Attenborough tells the story of Steve Biko's life?

3 Which comedian's catchphrase was 'You lucky people!'?

4 Who wrote the play *Inadmissible Evidence*?

5 What is the state capital of North Dakota?

1 Who in sport is known as 'the Whirlwind'?

2 What was Captain Bligh's rank at the time of the mutiny on the *Bounty*?

3 What was the name of the governor of Texas who was riding in the car with John F. Kennedy when he was assassinated?

4 Which city has the railway stations Snow Hill and New Street?

5 Which American film director directed John Wayne's *Stagecoach* and *The Man who Shot Liberty Valance*?

Q 8

ROUND 10   *Individual questions for team 2*

Sport
Which sport is associated with the Federation Cup?
Soap operas
In *Twin Peaks*, what was the name of the first murder victim?
England
Which London street is associated with the film industry?
Science
What theory states that nothing can be measured or observed without disturbing it?
Art
Which artist painted the well known 'Bubbles'?

Team 1	**Team 2**

DRINKS ROUND

1   From which Gilbert and Sullivan work comes 'I can't help it, I was born sneering'?

2   Who in 1978 made the record 'Take a Chance on Me'?

3   What is another, and Christian, name for Pentecost?

4   What begins with the vernal equinox?

5   Give the more common name for the plant *Convollaria majolis*, sometimes used to make perfume.

1   From which Gilbert and Sullivan work comes 'I'm very good at integral and differential calculus'?

2   Who in 1978 made the record 'Talking in Your Sleep'?

3   Why was Jesus of Nazareth a thaumaturgist?

4   In Scandinavian countries what are supposed to roam on Walpurgis Night?

5   Give the more common name for the low-growing *Myosotis* plant, which has blue, pink or white flowers.

Q 8

6 Suez lies at one end of the Suez Canal; which city lies at the other?

7 Who wrote published poems to Maud Gonne, though she finally refused to marry him?

8 Which country manufactured DAF cars?

9 Which actor progressed from *Pennies from Heaven* to *The Long Good Friday*?

10 Who was the founder of Rome?

6 Between which two of North America's great lakes do the Niagara Falls lie?

7 Who wrote *The Postman Always Rings Twice*?

8 Where does Limburger cheese come from?

9 Which musical, later made into a film, transferred the Gospel of St Matthew to a community of hippies in New York?

10 Which Roman road ran from Rome to Brindisi?

Q
8

RESERVE QUESTIONS

1 When did Britain adopt the Gregorian calendar? Answer to be within 20 years.

2 What 'blood messengers' are the product of the endocrine glands?

3 What was the family relationship of US presidents William Henry Harrison and Benjamin Harrison?

Pub League Quiz 9

The individual questions are in Rounds 5 and 10 and are on the following subjects: Television, Classical music, Law, General knowledge and Nicknames.

Team 1

ROUND 1

1 Which 1959 film was awarded 11 Oscars?

2 Who was the first Labour prime minister with an independent majority?

3 Which capital city stands on the Manzanares river?

4 In which English county would you find the Cheddar Gorge?

5 What type of creature is a nutcracker?

ROUND 2

1 Who is sometimes known as the 'godfather of soul'?

2 What is measured with an anemometer?

3 Which poem about a monster did Lewis Carroll's Alice read?

Team 2

1 Which actress won four Oscars between 1932 and 1981?

2 Name the Liberal politician who was succeeded by Jeremy Thorpe as Liberal leader in 1967.

3 Which capital city stands on the Potomac river?

4 What is another name for Shropshire county?

5 To which animal family do martens belong?

1 Which female soul singer issued the album 'Young, Gifted and Black' in 1972?

2 What does polyphonic mean?

3 In 'Jabberwocky', what did gyre and gimble in the wabe?

4 What in music is an interval?

4 What is the smallest interval on a piano called?

5 Who was responsible for the reform of the Carmelite order and died in 1582?

5 Who is the patron saint of Spain, a virgin martyr whose emblem is a lamb?

ROUND 3

1 From which film starring Jane Fonda did pop group Duran Duran get their name?

1 What was Elvis Presley's first motion picture?

2 What is the home of a hare called?

2 What is the home of an eagle called?

3 The Opium Wars in the Far East were mainly between which two countries?

3 Which country declared war on Britain on 18 June 1812?

4 Who was the merchant of Venice in Shakespeare's play?

4 Who was the moor of Venice in Shakespeare's play?

5 What is the state capital of Hawaii?

5 What is the state capital of California?

Q
9

ROUND 4

1 Whom did Jimmy Carter succeed as president of the USA?

1 Whom did Margaret Thatcher succeed as prime minister?

2 Who wrote Nancy Reagan's unauthorised biography in 1991?

2 Who wrote the celebrated book *Diana: Her True Story*?

3 How much is a 'sawbuck' in American slang?

3 What is gambling slang for £500 or $500?

4 Who gave Victoria Falls their name?

4 Columbus discovered the West Indies by mistake. Where did he originally set sail for?

5 What date is St Swithin's Day?

5 In what month does the Chelsea Flower Show normally take place?

ROUND 5 *Individual questions for team 1*

Television
In which quiz series did the Princess Royal participate?
Classical music
Which work by Vivaldi did Nigel Kennedy make a hit?
Law
Name two of the divisions of the legal year known as sittings.
General knowledge
Which publisher became chairman of Derby County Football Club?
Nicknames
What was General Joseph Stilwell's nickname?

Team 2 | *Team 1*

ROUND 6

1 Dundalk is the county town of Ireland's smallest county. What is the county?

1 In which Irish county would you find both the Curragh and much of the Bog of Allen?

2 Who first recorded the song 'I've Got You Babe'?

2 Which zither player provided *The Third Man* theme?

3 What name was given to Cromwell's troopers in the Civil War?

3 By what name are the yeoman warders of the Tower of London better known?

4 What do onomasticians study?

4 What is monotheism?

5 What is the oldest known alcoholic beverage?

5 What is a jeroboam?

ROUND 7

1 What planet has the satellite Nereid?

2 What is the name of the ghost ship that reputedly haunts the Cape of Good Hope?

3 Which is the first of the *Canterbury Tales*?

4 What is the distinctive feature of the proboscis monkey?

5 In which county is Stansted airport?

1 Triton is a satellite of which planet?

2 What is the name of the wizard who reputedly lived in a cave in Tintagel, Cornwall?

3 Which is the last of the *Canterbury Tales*?

4 Where in the world would you find budgerigars in their natural habitat?

5 What is the name of the home of the Chelsea Pensioners in London?

ROUND 8

1 From what cereal is sweetcorn made?

2 Who was the Greek god of time?

3 Who wrote the musical *Oliver*?

4 Who wrote *The Agony and the Ecstacy*?

5 Narcolepsy is the medical term for what?

1 What is fermented barley called?

2 Who was the Roman god of time?

3 From which musical does 'They Call The Wind Maria' come?

4 Who created Dr Fu Manchu?

5 What is acetylsalicylic acid better known as?

ROUND 9

1 Which famous British warship was sunk by the German battleship *Bismarck* in May 1941?

2 Where is *The Scotsman* newspaper printed?

1 What happened to the transatlantic liner *Lusitania*?

2 What daily newspaper was formerly the *Daily Worker*?

Q
9

3 Who was the first king of the Belgians?

4 Who fired blank shots at HM the Queen at the Trooping of the Colour ceremony in July 1981?

5 What make of car was advertised with the slogan *'Vorsprung durch technik'*?

3 Who was the first Stuart king of Scotland?

4 Whom did Mehmet Ali Agca try to assassinate on 13 May 1981?

5 With what perfume has Liz Hurley been associated professionally?

ROUND 10 *Individual questions for team 2*

Television
Which character was the oldest member of *Dad's Army*?
Classical music
Who composed the opera *Ruslan and Ludmilla*?
Law
What word means the 'philosophy of the law'?
General knowledge
What famous city is known to its residents as the Big Apple?
Nicknames
Which great Florentine artist is known to history by his nickname meaning 'little barrel'?

Q 9

Team 1

Team 2

DRINKS ROUND

1 Which country has sovereignty over the three Juan Fernandez islands?

2 Prunella Scales has appeared in *Coronation Street*. True or false?

3 For what was Sir Noel Murless noted?

1 What is Old Faithful in Yellowstone National Park, Wyoming?

2 *Pardon the Expression* is the only spin-off TV series of *Coronation Street*. True or false?

3 In which sport was Beryl Burton a prolific title holder?

4 Which liqueur bears the letters D.O.M. on the bottle label?

5 What ruined Cistercian abbey is eight miles north of Harrogate?

6 A name for Tommy Handley's radio series was *I.T.M.A.* What did this stand for?

7 Whom did Rocky Marciano defeat to become heavyweight champion of the world?

8 Who was 'Uncle Mac'?

9 In which county is Flodden Field?

10 What is Margaret Thatcher's middle name?

4 What kind of drink is a negus?

5 Which famous zoo would you find near Dunstable?

6 Which British comedian portrayed the incompetent school-master of St Michael's on stage and screen?

7 Which famous singer from Rochdale spent most of her later life on the island of Capri?

8 Who was the 'Forces' Sweetheart'?

9 In which county are the Quantock Hills?

10 The first Lord Stockton died in 1986. By what name will he be most remembered?

Q
9

RESERVE QUESTIONS

1 Who are the only two commoners in English history to be honoured with a state funeral?

2 Which national flag has vertical stripes of gold and blue, with a black trident in the centre?

3 Which Hollywood film-maker developed the concept of the 'silly symphony'?

Pub League Quiz 10

The individual questions are in Rounds 5 and 10 and are on the following subjects: In common, Name the year, Pop music, Religion and Pot luck.

Team 1

ROUND 1

1 What word meaning literally 'our father' describes the Lord's Prayer recited in Latin?

2 In which country are the Vosges mountains?

3 In which year did Luna 9 make a soft landing on the moon, Malawi become a republic, talks on Rhodesia on board HMS *Tiger* begin, and was Dr Verwoerd of South Africa assassinated?

4 What was the initial occupation of the Italian dictator Benito Mussolini?

5 How many balls are there on the table at the start of a game of snooker?

Team 2

1 How many beads are there on a rosary?

2 Mount Aconcagua in South America is over 23,000 ft high. In which country is it situated?

3 John Francis attempted the assassination of which British monarch?

4 Mahatma Gandhi qualified in England for which profession before practising in South Africa?

5 What is the name of the game which resembles billiards and is played with numbered cups instead of pockets?

ROUND 2

1 Name one of the two events celebrated by the flying of the Union Flag on government buildings each year on 10 March.

2 What did Noel Gallagher and Liam Gallagher form in Manchester in 1993?

3 Which bird has 'eyes' in its tail?

4 Who was the first Duke of Marlborough?

5 In what game are the Bermuda Bowl and the Venice Trophy major competitions?

1 Name the three children of the Prince of Monaco.

2 Which comedy duo had a Number 1 hit in 1991 with 'The Stonk'?

3 Which fabulous bird arose from its own ashes?

4 At which battle of 1704 did he defeat the French and Bavarians?

5 K1, K2, C1 and C2 are classes of competition in which sport?

ROUND 3

1 Two numbers add up to 54 and there is 12 between them. What are they?

2 Name one of the islands off the coast of Malta.

3 Who was the first man to swim the English Channel?

1 If one number is three times another and their difference is 10, what are they?

2 Which country has common borders with Argentina, Bolivia and Brazil?

3 Which sport originated in India and is played on the largest pitch of any ball game in the world?

Q 10

4 Which team were the first ever winners of the Football League Cup?

5 Who crushed Monmouth's rebellion in 1685?

ROUND 4

1 What does *in toto* mean?

2 Who was the first Director-general of the BBC 1927–1938?

3 On what river does York stand?

4 What was the special skill of the biblical Ishmael, son of Abraham?

5 LOT is the national airline of which country?

4 Name two of the three clubs Graham Souness played for before he became player-manager of Glasgow Rangers.

5 What dynasty of kings descended from Pepin the Short?

1 What does *id est* mean?

2 Which West Indian cricketer became a governor of the BBC?

3 On what river does Harrogate stand?

4 What sign of the zodiac is represented by an archer?

5 Which country puts *Magyar Posta* on its stamps?

ROUND 5   *Individual questions for team 1*

Q 10

In common
What did James Madison, John Quincy Adams, James Polk and Ulysses S. Grant have in common?
Name the year
In which year did Israel become independent?
Pop music
Who had five successive Number 1 hit singles in the USA, beginning with 'Visions of Love'?
Religion
What is another word for carol singing?
Pot luck
Give the full title of the Bishop of Bath.

Team 2	**Team 1**

ROUND 6

1	How does the male cricket chirp?
2	In the world of international alliances, what is the OAU?
3	In which county is Arundel Castle?
4	What name is given to the sign of conferring a knighthood where the sovereign touches the knight with the flat of the sword?
5	What is a slow-worm?

Team 1

1	How does a humming bird hum?
2	What does NFU stand for?
3	Which stately home, with designs by Holbein and Inigo Jones, is the seat of the earls of Pembroke?
4	Name the famous theatre in Dublin founded in 1904, for plays written by Irish playwrights and performed by Irish actors.
5	What name is given to animals that suckle their young?

ROUND 7

Team 2

1	What part does the Honourable Susan Nicholls play in *Coronation Street*?
2	What in heraldry is a broad, horizontal strip across the middle of a shield?
3	Who wrote *The Count of Monte Cristo*?
4	Name the main Moscow news agency.

Team 1

1	In *Soap*, what was the name of the Tates' original butler?
2	What is the heraldic term for full-faced?
3	Who wrote the novel *The Moon and Sixpence*?
4	What was the capital of unoccupied France in 1940?

5 What school did Billy Bunter attend?

5 Who was the storyteller in the tales of Brer Rabbit?

ROUND 8

1 On which river do the cities of Quebec and Montreal stand?

2 What kind of birds are rock, cushat and stock?

3 Who was the second US president?

4 By what creature was the Greek god Adonis killed?

5 What is the state capital of Tasmania?

1 In which US state is the Grand Canyon?

2 Name the Australian wild dog.

3 Who was the first US president?

4 Which queen is supposed to have founded Carthage?

5 Which capital city stands on the Dambovita river?

ROUND 9

1 Who was poet laureate from 1843 to 1850?

2 In which battle of 1346 did the English defeat the French though outnumbered by at least two to one?

3 What was written by the finger of God on two tablets of stone on Mount Sinai?

4 What is tapioca made from?

5 What name is given to any substance which speeds up a chemical reaction, but itself remains unchanged?

1 Who was poet laureate from 1930 to 1967?

2 Which English king was the leader of the Third Crusade with Philip II of France?

3 What is the general name for the first four books of the New Testament?

4 What is semolina derived from?

5 Name the colourless inert gas isolated by Daniel Rutherford in 1772, that has the symbol N.

ROUND 10   *Individual questions for team 2*

In common
Entrechat, glissade, pas seul and *fouetté* are all terms in which art?

Name the year
Name the year George Brown resigned as foreign secretary, Yuri Gagarin was killed and Martin Luther King was assassinated.

Pop music
Which pop singer became Yusuf Islam?

Religion
Name the most sacred of all holy places in the Jewish religion.

Pot luck
Who was the playwright whose first play was *Widowers' Houses*, who won the 1925 Nobel Prize for literature and declined a peerage?

Team 1	Team 2

DRINKS ROUND

1   From which musical does the song 'Luck Be A Lady' come?

1   From which musical does the song 'My Funny Valentine' come?

2   By what other names are the constellations *Corona Australis* and *Corona Borealis* better known?

2   In which direction does a comet's tail always point?

3   Who murdered Martin Luther King?

3   Who murdered Mahatma Gandhi?

4   What on a boat are scuppers?

4   What on a boat is the taffrail?

5   If, on New Year's Day, it is 12 noon GMT, what is the time in Paris?

5   If, on New Year's Day, it is 12 noon GMT, what is the time in New York?

6 Which German artist at the age of 13 drew the first self-portrait in European history, using a mirror?

7 What colour is a moonstone?

8 What does omniscient mean?

9 In which month did the Romans celebrate the feast of Saturnalia?

10 Who was the Oscar-winning star in *Gandhi*?

6 Which artist worked for the Elector of Saxony and is still famous for his woodcuts and copperplates?

7 Give another name for a bloodstone.

8 What is an acronym?

9 The Emperor Claudius had his wife executed for entering a bigamous marriage. What was her name?

10 Who was the Oscar-winning star in *Cabaret*?

RESERVE QUESTIONS

1 Enrico Caruso was regarded as the greatest singer of his day. Was he a tenor, baritone or bass?

2 *Borstal Boy* is the autobiography of which Irish playwright?

3 Which Italian striker joined Middlesbrough for £7 million in July 1996?

Q 10

Pub League Quiz 11

The individual questions are in Rounds 5 and 10 and are on the following subjects: Films, Plants and wildlife, Dates, Sport and General knowledge.

Team 1

ROUND 1

1   What is the name of the police station in *The Bill*?

2   In which European country is the parliament called the *Eduskunta*?

3   Who wrote *The Hitchhiker's Guide to the Galaxy*?

4   What does RAAF stand for?

5   Which great city used to be called New Amsterdam?

ROUND 2

1   In which film did the director's father co-star with Humphrey Bogart?

2   What relation was Henry II of England to Henry I?

Team 2

ROUND 1

1   What is the name of the town defended by *Dad's Army*?

2   Name the Irish nationalist with whom Gladstone came to terms and introduced the Home Rule Bill in 1886.

3   *Stamp Album* is a book by which actor?

4   What does CGS stand for in the armed forces?

5   What was the name of Volgograd from 1925 to 1961?

ROUND 2

1   Peter Sellers starred in the film *What's New Pussycat?* Who wrote the script?

2   How many of William the Conqueror's sons became kings of England? Name them.

Q
11

3 Which film star's legs were insured for a million dollars by Twentieth Century Fox?

4 What has the atomic number 1?

5 What was the food of the Greek gods?

ROUND 3

1 Who became secretary-general of NATO in 1984?

2 What is *sauerkraut*?

3 Name The Who's rock opera.

4 What was the heroine's name in the book *A Room with a View*?

5 In the board game, what does the word Ludo mean?

ROUND 4

1 Name three of the four great estuaries of England.

2 In which country was Bonnie Tyler lost?

3 Who baptised Jesus?

4 What was known as the 'royal disease'?

3 Who said, suggesting a well-known phrase, 'a sex symbol becomes an object. I hate being an object'?

4 What has the atomic number 2?

5 What was the drink of the Greek gods?

1 Who was chancellor of the exchequer in 1974?

2 What is the singular of scampi?

3 Who wrote 'Maple Leaf Rag' in 1897?

4 What did the owl and the pussycat eat with a runcible spoon?

5 How many murder weapons are there in the game of Cluedo?

1 Name the highest peaks of England, Scotland, Wales and Ireland (three of the four required).

2 Which state was on Ray Charles's mind?

3 In which river was Jesus baptised?

4 What is the common name for the disease trypanosomiasis?

5 What tropical mammal related to the cat has a perfume gland in the groin?

5 The chihuahua is a native of which country?

ROUND 5 *Individual questions for team 1*

Films
Which was Roger Moore's first Bond film?
Plants and wildlife
What is esparto?
Dates
Of the years 1800, 1900 and 2000, which is a leap year?
Sport
Which French boxer was national champion in every weight and division before becoming light heavyweight champion of the world in 1920?
General knowledge
What is the adult leader of a Brownie pack called?

Team 2	*Team 1*

ROUND 6

1 Which two books by Charles Dickens were written in the first person?

1 Which two characters from *The Army Game* had a comedy series of their own?

Q 11

2 How many sides does a nonagon have?

2 In which science would you find the concept of final or marginal utility?

3 What is agoraphobia?

3 What is megalomania?

4 Who was quoted as saying, 'My advice if you insist on slimming: eat as much as you like – just don't swallow it'?

4 Who was quoted as saying, 'If all the young ladies attending it (the Yale Prom) were laid end to end, I wouldn't be at all surprised'?

5 In which fictional village is *Peak Practice* set?

5 Who stars opposite Richard Wilson in *One Foot in the Grave*?

ROUND 7

1 Which country's flag is a blue cross on a white background?

1 In which country can you salute a national flag which is different on one side from the other?

2 What have Leighton Rees, Keith Deller, Bob Anderson and Phil Taylor all won?

2 Who succeeded John Francome as National Hunt champion jockey?

3 What is the chemical symbol for phosphorus?

3 What is the most common natural ore of aluminium in the world?

4 In which film did Marilyn Monroe co-star with Laurence Olivier?

4 In which 1962 film did Alec Guinness portray King Faisal?

5 In which group of Scottish islands is the Old Man of Hoy?

5 On which Scottish island is Stornoway?

ROUND 8

1 In which year was Prince Charles born?

1 What did Albert, Duke of York become?

2 Which city is the home of the Hallé Orchestra?

2 What craft is the town of Cluny in France famous for?

3 Who was the first black boxer to win the world heavyweight title?

3 To whom did Henry Cooper lose his British heavyweight title in 1971?

4 From which poem is the line, 'The curfew tolls the knell of parting day'?

4 From which poem is the line, 'If I should die think only this of me'?

5 Which countries are divided by the 38th parallel?

5 Which countries are divided by the 49th parallel?

ROUND 9

1 Who was executed before the Banqueting Hall in Whitehall on 30 January 1649?

1 Which children's book character was always saying, 'Off with his head'?

2 Who recorded the 1959 hit record 'Living Doll'?

2 Who wrote 'Living Doll'?

3 What was the famous book that James Hilton wrote about the life of a schoolmaster, later made into a film?

3 Muriel Spark wrote a book about a head-strong schoolmistress, which was made into a film. What was it called?

4 Where did the German fleet mutiny in October 1918?

4 What battle, in May 1942, saved Australia from invasion by the Japanese?

5 How many points is the letter 'B' worth in Scrabble?

5 If a bingo caller shouts 'Two fat ladies', what number has been drawn?

ROUND 10   *Individual questions for team 2*

Films
Who directed the film *E.T.: The Extra-Terrestrial?*

Q
11

Plants and wildlife
Which crop is susceptible to the Colorado beetle?

Dates
What heavenly body determines the date of Easter?

Sport
Where were the first Commonwealth Games held?

General knowledge
What, is it said, did President Santa Anna of Mexico keep in his hacienda from 1838 until its ceremonial burial in 1842?

Team 1	Team 2

DRINKS ROUND

1 Whose husbands were Louis VII of France and Henry II of England?

1 What monarch was the son of Mary, Queen of Scots and Lord Darnley?

2 On which estuary is the town of Chatham?

2 Of which range of chalk hills is Haddington Hill, near Wendover, a part?

3 In which country is the mountain range Sierra Madre?

3 In which country is the mountain range Sierra Morena?

4 What are grown in the following forms? Fan, standard, cordon and espalier.

4 What are made in the following forms? Fly, chain, feather and whipping?

5 Who wrote the plays *Uncle Vanya* and *The Three Sisters*?

5 Which Verdi opera was based on Victor Hugo's play *Le Roi s'amuse*?

6 How does the Bishop of Rochester sign himself?

6 How does the Bishop of Carlisle sign himself?

7 UNITA was dedicated to gaining the independence of which Portuguese colony?

7 In what part of the world is Quechua still spoken?

8 Which broadcaster famously threw a glass of wine over Jonathan Aitken?

8 On which factual TV programme do Jill Dando and Nick Ross form a team?

9 Where was Napoleon Bonaparte born?

9 Where in Italy was Leonardo da Vinci born?

10 Which river flows through Hamburg and Dresden?

10 Which country beginning with the letter 'A' does not end with that letter?

Q 11

RESERVE QUESTIONS

1 What part of the body may be affected by nephritis?
2 Pandit Nehru and his daugher Indira were the first and third prime ministers of independent India. Who was the second?
3 Which bandleader had the signature tune 'One o'Clock Jump'?

Q
11

Pub League Quiz 12

The individual questions are in Rounds 5 and 10 and are on the following subjects: Sport, Art and artists, Nobel Prize winners, Composers and English monarchs.

Team 1

Team 2

ROUND 1

1 In what year did the series of modern Olympic Games begin?

2 What was Linus Yale's occupation?

3 Name the only book written by Margaret Mitchell.

4 Who, in an act of bravery, walked out of Scott's tent?

5 Which girl were Simon and Garfunkel singing about with the line, 'You're shaking my confidence daily'?

1 Which city hosted the first Winter Olympics to be held in Asia?

2 What invention of Jacob Schick could be said to have changed the face of man when it appeared in 1931?

3 Which author disappeared after *The Murder of Roger Ackroyd*?

4 To which movement did the heroes and heroines of World War 2's *Maquis* belong?

5 Who sang about Lily the Pink's invention of medicinal compound?

ROUND 2

1 Practically all of the Kalahari Desert is in which country?

2 Who was awarded a four-pound gold soccer ball after scoring his 1,000th goal?

1 Which two countries lie either side of the Thar Desert?

2 In which ball game did Geoffrey B. Hunt of Australia rise to become world champion?

3 Which chemical has the symbol Mg?

4 Which six-letter English word means to stick fast as well as meaning the complete opposite?

5 On which continent did early man first develop, according to most scientists?

3 Ra are the letters which represent which element?

4 There is only one genuine English word which ends in the letters 'amt'. What is it?

5 In which African country is Lake Turkana, famous for its remains of early man?

ROUND 3

1 Who wrote *The Alchemist*?

2 In transport, what does APT stand for?

3 What did Heinrich Dreser introduce into medicine in 1893?

4 How many gallons are there in a bushel?

5 In which country is Biskra?

1 Who wrote *The Mill on the Floss*?

2 What does BAOR stand for?

3 What did shop proprietor James Ritty patent in 1879?

4 How many gallons are there in a peck?

5 In which country is Beisan?

ROUND 4

1 What is a ruminant?

2 Which of the boulevards in Paris links the Arc de Triomphe and Place de la Concorde?

3 What do Robert Hayes, James Hines and Armin Hary have in common?

1 What is a mendicant?

2 In which American thoroughfare is the White House?

3 In what sphere of athletic sport was Sergey Litvinov a champion?

Q 12

4 What is Robin Good-fellow known as in *A Midsummer Night's Dream*?

5 Who played Ma Boswell in *Bread*?

4 Which of Shakespeare's heroines speaks the lines, 'O brave new world, that has such people in it'?

5 Which entertainer's real name is Cherilyn Sarkisian?

ROUND 5   *Individual questions for team 1*

Sport
What game would you be playing if you were competing for the Swaythling Cup?

Art and artists
What was Rubens' first name?

Nobel Prize winners
Who declined the Nobel Peace Prize shared with Henry Kissinger in 1973?

Composers
Who wrote the *Sea Symphony*?

English monarchs
Who became king when Henry VI was overthrown in 1461?

Team 2	Team 1

ROUND 6

1 From which country do Walloons come?

2 In what liquid does a cook coddle eggs?

3 How many stars make up Orion's belt?

4 In which present-day country was Erasmus born?

1 In which country will you find the Swiss Guard?

2 Where are a flatfish's eyes?

3 Which of the planets is nearest to the sun?

4 In which country was Albert Einstein born?

Q
12

5 Which Peter Shaffer play is about a boy who blinds horses?

5 In which play is Lydia Languish courted by Jack Absolute?

ROUND 7

1 Which South American country had an inflation rate of over 8,000 per cent in 1985?

1 In which South American city, and present-day country, was Simon Bolivar born?

2 Which was the first country to host both the Summer and the Winter Olympics in the same year?

2 Which British athlete won a gold medal in that year, in the Summer Olympics 400 metres event?

3 The fry of which fish is served up as whitebait?

3 Which fish, olive brown with black spots, has a distinctive barbel at each side of its mouth?

4 Which particular art form did Alexander Calder invent and exhibit in the 1930s?

4 A group of American landscape painters which included Samuel Morse, was named after a river. Which was it?

5 Which country did Pol Pot terrorise?

5 Which secret society was dedicated to driving European settlers out of Kenya?

ROUND 8

1 Which TV series featured Cpl. Rocco Barbella?

1 Which British TV series inspired the American series *All in the Family*?

2 Anne, Dick, George and Julian were four of Enid Blyton's 'Famous Five'. Who was the fifth?

2 Name the famous actor who has children named Hayley, Jonathan and Juliet.

Q 12

3 Who signed an auto-graph for his killer shortly before he was assassinated in New York?

4 Who wrote the play *Hedda Gabler*?

5 Which is the oldest of the Bowl games played in American college football?

3 In which city was Mrs 'Cory' Aquino's husband assassinated?

4 Who wrote the autobiographical play *Long Day's Journey into Night*?

5 In which stadium do the Miami Dolphins play their home games?

ROUND 9

1 What did John Hawkins start selling to New World settlers in 1562?

2 Which author won the Pulitzer Prize for fiction in 1952 for *The Caine Mutiny*?

3 Who ended Bjorn Borg's run of five successive Wimbledon singles titles?

4 Who discovered radio waves in 1887?

5 What was the name of the hypnotising musician in Gerald du Maurier's *Trilby*?

1 Which country was the first to have universal suffrage?

2 Which author won the Pulitzer Prize for fiction in 1953 for *The Old Man and the Sea*?

3 How many players are there on each side in Australian Rules football?

4 Which Briton patented car disc brakes in 1902?

5 Name the film starring Ingrid Bergman which was adapted from the book *The Small Woman*.

Q
12

ROUND 10 *Individual questions for team 2*

Sport
What do the Sheffield Steelers play?
Art and artists
Which artist had the forenames Joseph Mallord William?
Nobel Prize winners
Which organisation won the Nobel Peace Prize in 1965?
Composers
Which composer's first opera was *Orfeo*?
English monarchs
Who was king before Edward the Confessor?

Team 1	Team 2

DRINKS ROUND

1 Which show from the City Varieties in Leeds was screened for over 30 years?

2 Which trio had a hit with 'Baby Love'?

3 What race in England is over a distance of four miles, one furlong and 180 yards?

4 Where is the setting for John le Carre's *A Small Town in Germany*?

5 Which country is the home of the sweet wine called Tokay?

6 Which planet did Viking 1 land on?

1 What TV show was broadcast for the first time at 6.30 a.m. on 17 January 1983?

2 Which UK duo had a hit with 'I Know Him So Well'?

3 What is a good mudder likely to win in the US?

4 Which country provides the setting for the novel *Summer of the Seventeenth Doll*?

5 What is the technical term for new wine, or grape juice, before fermentation is complete?

6 Which planet did the Mariner 2, 9 and 10 spacecraft explore?

Q 12

7 Which animal in Aesop's fable assumed the grapes he couldn't reach were sour anyway?

8 What name is given to an enthusiast of all things French?

9 What was the name of the horse made a consul by Emperor Caligula?

10 Who created the imaginary language Newspeak?

7 How did Apollo punish the prophetess Cassandra?

8 What is phagophobia?

9 What is the name of Clint Eastwood's orangutan film co-star?

10 Who created the imaginary place Blefuscu?

RESERVE QUESTIONS

1 What is the unit of currency in Pakistan?

2 What vaccine preceded Sabin vaccine in the fight against polio?

3 Which Greek philosopher founded his own Academy at Athens?

Q 12

Pub League Quiz 13

The individual questions are in Rounds 5 and 10 and are on the following subjects: Famous people, Films, Wars, The Ancients and Plant life.

Team 1	Team 2

ROUND 1

1 Which is the world's largest gulf?

1 What region covers Norway, Sweden, Finland and Russia within the Arctic Circle?

2 In the nursery rhyme, what was the only tune that Tom, the piper's son, could play?

2 In the nursery rhyme 'Pease Porridge Hot', how old was the porridge?

3 Which press tycoon did Marion Davies keep company with for over 30 years?

3 Which Christine nearly brought down the British government in the Profumo scandal of 1963?

4 What was Jeeves' given name?

4 Who wrote about Mr Polly and Mr Britling?

5 To which parts of the human body does the word 'volar' relate?

5 What is the hardest substance in the human body?

ROUND 2

1 Which country is named after the line of latitude that runs through it?

1 Which South American country took its name from the Latin for 'silvery'?

2 Which film had Mia Farrow and John Cassavetes facing the prospects of bringing up a little devil?

2 Which film booted 'Singin' in the Rain' back into cinema in 1971?

Q 13

3 Don and Phil were brothers who made up which singing duo?

4 Who was England's first official poet laureate?

5 How long is a tennis court from baseline to baseline?

3 Ray Davis and Dave Davis were brothers in which pop group?

4 From which poem are these lines, 'Laugh, and the world laughs with you; Weep, and you weep alone'?

5 How high is the net on a tennis court, at the centre?

ROUND 3

1 Which religion was founded by Guru Nanak?

2 What was the name of P.T. Barnum's famous elephant?

3 What is removal of tissue from a living body for diagnostic purposes called?

4 What does the word Esperanto actually mean?

5 How is 2,000 written in Roman numerals?

1 What is the principal religion of the island of Bali?

2 Which US army horse survived after Custer's last stand?

3 What word describes the region of earth, air and water inhabited by living organisms?

4 What does the word *kamikaze* mean?

5 What number cannot be represented by Roman numerals?

ROUND 4

1 What is the correct title of the daughter of an earl, marquis or duke?

2 In which country are the ruins of Troy?

3 From where does the Kirov Ballet come?

1 What is the correct title of the wife of a knight or baronet?

2 Where in China are the famous terracotta soldiers?

3 Who founded what is now the Royal Ballet?

Q 13

| **4** What are the highest odds paid by a casino in a roulette game? | **4** What is the highest score possible from a single stroke at billiards? |
| **5** What is the most sacred river in India? | **5** By what name is the former colony of the Belgian Congo now known? |

ROUND 5 *Individual questions for team 1*

Famous people
In which field of the arts did Jacob Epstein achieve fame?
Films
Who directed the film *Apocalypse Now*?
Wars
Which war did the Potsdam Conference follow?
The Ancients
Who was chained to a mountain where an eagle tore at his liver every day?
Plant life
What plant, with a stem of up to a foot, and droopy, pale green flowers, has a stinking variety?

| **Team 2** | **Team 1** |

ROUND 6
1 Which is the world's highest navigable lake?	**1** What port, Israel's only outlet to the Red Sea, stands at the head of the Gulf of Aqaba?
2 Who won an Oscar as best actor, in *Coming Home*?	**2** Who won an Oscar as best actress, in *Coming Home*?
3 In which country was the Boxer Rebellion?	**3** In which country did the Battle of Waterloo take place?
4 Who is the subject of Irving Stone's *Lust for Life*?	**4** Which Hermann Hesse book gave its name to a rock group?

Q
13

91

5 What caused over 20 million deaths worldwide, in the years 1918 and 1919?

5 Worldwide, which is the most common blood group?

ROUND 7

1 What is the usual diameter of a golf hole?

1 In golf, what name is given to an intended stroke where the player misses the ball altogether?

2 What is another name for a concertina?

2 How was a dulcimer played?

3 What is the surname of the Bee Gees?

3 What is the surname of the Beach Boys?

4 Who wrote *The Alexandria Quartet*?

4 Whose first novel was *This Sporting Life*?

5 What colour is a Remy Martin bottle?

5 What makes up a Black Velvet?

ROUND 8

1 Who moved from Radio Luxembourg to Radio 1, where his breakfast show was a great success from 1972 to 1977?

1 What replaced Roy Hattersley when he failed to turn up for his scheduled TV appearance on *Have I Got News For You*?

2 Which Carthaginian general had both a brother and a brother-in-law named Hasdrubal?

2 Whom did the Athenians defeat at the Battle of Marathon?

3 Where is Waikiki beach?

3 Which fictional character was born Jimmy Gatz and had a mansion on Long Island?

4 Where in North Carolina did the first powered flight by the Wright brothers take place?

4 Who piloted the Hughes H4 Hercules, the largest aeroplane ever flown, when it made its one flight in 1947?

5 Which sport features a movement called a veronica?

5 In which sport is the goal called a hail?

ROUND 9

1 Which Mediterranean island was celebrated in antiquity for its copper mines?

1 Which group of islands carries the Danish name that means 'sheep' in English?

2 Name the lead singer with Guns 'n' Roses.

2 Who was the original lead singer with the Pogues?

3 What event is celebrated on 14 July in France?

3 What feast, held on 6 January, celebrates the manifestation of Christ's divinity to the Magi?

4 What soap was initially entitled *Dynasty II*?

4 In *Cheers,* what is Sam Malone's nickname?

5 What puts the fizz in soda water?

5 How many grams make a pound (within five grams)?

ROUND 10   *Individual questions for team 2*

Famous people
Who organised the Transglobe expedition of 1979–82 which traced the Greenwich meridian crossing both Poles?

Q
13

Films
Which 1973 film was based on a bestseller by the novelist William Peter Blatty?

Wars
Which war ended the Austrian-Hungarian monarchy?

The Ancients
Which ancient civilisation believed that an eclipse was caused by a dragon trying to eat the sun?
Plant life
Which fungus has a crown, spores, gills and a stalk?

Team 1	Team 2

DRINKS ROUND

1 Which Australian prime minister disappeared while swimming, in 1967?

2 Who changed groups from the Faces to the Rolling Stones?

3 What nationality is the 100 metres sprint star Donovan Bailey?

4 What cocktail is made from vodka, Galliano and orange juice?

5 What were 'Babe' Ruth's given names?

6 In the Bible, how long did Jonah spend in the belly of the whale?

7 From which language do we get the words catamaran and curry?

1 Which Australian starred in the film *Grease*?

2 Whose first hit was 'Your Song'?

3 Who was disqualified from the Olympic 100 metres final of 1996 after two false starts?

4 Vodka and lime juice are two of the main ingredients of a Moscow Mule. What is the third?

5 What were Jack Hobbs' given names?

6 What ancient book recounts Jewish folklore and the exploits of national heroes?

7 From which language do we get the words gingham and sarong?

Q 13

8 How many properties are there on a Monopoly board?

8 How many cards does each player have at the start of a game of pinochle?

9 What fell on 15 February 1942?

9 What burned on 27 February 1933?

10 Who played Captain Kirk in *Star Trek*?

10 Who, on TV, played the leading role in *I Claudius*?

RESERVE QUESTIONS

1 On which bay does the French resort of Biarritz lie?

2 In what mental illness does the sufferer believe, wrongly, that they are being persecuted by others, and may have delusions of grandeur?

3 What does an ammeter measure?

Q 13

Pub League Quiz 14

The individual questions are in Rounds 5 and 10 and are on the following subjects: Characters, International affairs, Disasters, Horses and courses and Inventions.

Team 1

ROUND 1
1 What is the largest island in Greece?
2 *Pelléus et Mélisande* is which composer's only opera?
3 Who played the part of Batman in the 1966 film?
4 Which species of gull, found on British coasts, spits foul-smelling oil onto its nest to protect it?
5 In what sport are 'rings' a class of competition?

ROUND 2
1 In which American state, according to an early Bee Gees hit, did the lights go out?
2 Who played the part of a gunslinging robot in *Futureworld*?

Team 2

1 Which is the largest island of Europe?
2 Which Verdi opera is based on the story of *The Lady of the Camellias*?
3 Who played the part of Joker in the *Batman* film of 1966?
4 What is most common domestic bird in the world?
5 In international boxing, what is now the lightest weight division?

1 Who in a recording of 1963, asked Long-distance Information about someone in Memphis, Tennessee?
2 Who starred in both *Trainspotting* and *The Full Monty*?

3 How many nights are there in the *Arabian Nights*?

4 What is a pennyroyal?

5 Which well-known snooker player carried the Olympic torch at the 1956 Olympics?

3 How many people took refuge in Noah's Ark?

4 What is the more usual name of the carnivorous plant also called a wake-robin or lords-and-ladies?

5 In 1965, for the first time in the twentieth century, two brothers played in the same England soccer team. Who were they?

ROUND 3

1 Whom did Peeping Tom peep at?

2 'Red-Green Gardens', first exhibited in 1921, was the work of which Swiss painter?

3 What is the world's most common compound?

4 In what field of sport is Chris Boardman a star performer?

5 Which country has the most land frontiers?

1 Who, according to ancient legends, holds up the sky?

2 Which Spanish artist is said to have promised to eat his wife after her death?

3 By what fraction of its volume does water expand when it freezes? Is it 1/5, 1/7, 1/8, 1/11 or 1/15?

4 At what game is Mike Russell a champion?

5 Which European frontier is only one and a half kilometres long?

ROUND 4

1 Who created the detective Albert Campion?

1 Who plays private investigator Hetty Wainthropp?

Q 14

2 Who wrote the lyrics for the film *Carmen Jones*?

3 Which J.M. Barrie character said, 'To die will be an awfully big adventure'?

4 Which of the five senses develops first?

5 Which is the largest city in Latin America?

2 Who wrote the music for *Porgy and Bess*?

3 Who wrote, 'If you can keep your head when all about you are losing theirs…you'll be a man, my son'?

4 Where is the human skin least sensitive?

5 What is the smallest Latin American country?

ROUND 5 *Individual questions for team 1*

Characters
Who was landlady to Sherlock Holmes?

International affairs
What did America buy for $7.2 million in 1867?

Disasters
Where did two jumbo jets collide in 1977, killing 574 people?

Horses and courses
Which horse won the Grand National in 1973, 1974 and 1977 and came second in 1975 and 1976?

Inventions
What form of camera did Edwin Land invent?

Team 2	*Team 1*

ROUND 6

1 In which American state is Michigan City?

2 Who was a policeman in Kansas before becoming a lawman in Tombstone, Arizona?

3 From what German coin does the dollar get its name?

1 Of which country is Jakarta the capital?

2 Which Hollywood actor was the most decorated soldier in US history?

3 What is the Chinese word for tea?

Q
14

4 What is 70 per cent of 70?

5 What is a shark's skeleton made of?

ROUND 7

1 If a dish is described as *parmentier*, which vegetable will be part of it?

2 Which London museum was founded in 1753 and opened to the public in 1759?

3 Name one of the two artists with whom Barbra Streisand had Number 1 hits?

4 What is the subject of the famous book written by English sage and astrologer Nicholas Culpeper?

5 The Prisoner declared in the cult TV series, 'I am not a number, I am a free man.' What number had he been assigned?

ROUND 8

1 Who played Marlon Brando's elder brother in *On the Waterfront*?

2 Which member of the cat family is unable to retract its claws?

4 How many years make up a vicennial period?

5 What does a whale shark feed on?

1 Which fish is traditionally eaten by Poles on Christmas Eve?

2 Who was kept in the Bastille from 1698 until his death in 1703?

3 Which father and daughter had a Number 1 hit?

4 Which annual first appeared in 1697 and has been published every year since?

5 What was the name of the priceless painting in *'Allo, 'Allo*?

1 Which actor led the expedition in the film *Journey to the Centre of the Earth*?

2 Which American mammal is distinguished by a black face-mark?

Q 14

3 In *Les Misérables*, what was Jean Valjean's first crime?

4 Name the supertanker which ran aground off the coast of Brittany in March 1978.

5 Which of Puccini's heroines is a famous singer?

ROUND 9

1 What form of transport is a *felucca*?

2 Which Englishman was both knighted and canonised, and was executed in 1535?

3 Which prime minister was also president of the MCC?

4 Who wrote a poem which begins, 'Remember me when I am gone away'?

5 Which country's parliament is called the *Folketing*?

3 What was the name of the Jew of Malta in Marlowe's play?

4 Which organisation won the Nobel Peace Prize in 1977?

5 Who wrote symphonies called the *Surprise*, the *Military*, the *Clock*, the *Drum-roll*, the *London* and the *Oxford*?

1 Who was the first person to reach a speed of 600 m.p.h. on land?

2 Which US president introduced prohibition?

3 Where is Sabina Park cricket ground?

4 Which bird is referred to in the line, 'Thou was't not born for death, immortal Bird!'?

5 To which branch of Protestantism do the religious majority in Finland belong?

Q 14

ROUND 10 *Individual questions for team 2*

Characters
What army did Shaw's Major Barbara serve in?
International affairs
Which incident prompted the installation of the 'hot line'?
Disasters
Which Australian city was devastated by Cyclone Tracy on Christmas Day 1974?
Horses and courses
Over what distance is the 2000 Guineas at Newmarket run?
Inventions
What household object did Percy LeBaron Spencer invent in 1945?

Team 1	*Team 2*

DRINKS ROUND

1 In which seaway are the Thousand Islands?

1 Which strait lies between Iceland and Greenland?

2 Which cricket side has as its emblem six martlets?

2 Who was bowling when Gary Sobers hit his famous six sixes?

3 Who seized power from King Idris after a coup in 1969?

3 Who succeeded Khruschev as USSR premier in 1964?

4 In which film did Spencer Tracy play a one-armed stranger?

4 In which Hitchcock film does Paul Newman play a scientist?

5 Who wrote *Portrait of the Artist as a Young Man*?

5 Who wrote *Portrait of the Artist as a Young Dog*?

6 In a bottle of wine what is the ullage?

6 What is the sediment at the bottom of a cask of wine called?

Q 14

7 What is Max Bygraves' real forename?

7 Which comedian's real name is Charles Springall?

8 Which former car factory worker earned a living at the post office in *Emmerdale*?

9 In which country is there a province called Luxembourg?

10 What is the smallest British mammal?

8 Which *Coronation Street* barmaid's first marriage lasted only a few days before she found solace in the arms of Des Barnes?

9 Where is the island of Rum?

10 Which shrew-like marsupial is native to Australia, Tasmania and New Guinea?

RESERVE QUESTIONS
1 What is H_2SO_4?
2 Who was the famous pupil of Anne Sullivan?
3 What did Lloyd George describe as Mr Balfour's poodle?

Q 14

The Answers

Pub League Quiz 1 Answers

Team 1

Team 2

ROUND 1

	Team 1		Team 2
1	The Nuba.	1	Their height. They are the world's tallest tribe.
2	Northern Australia.	2	Cook Strait.
3	Dirk Bogarde.	3	Bob Hope
4	November.	4	23 April.
5	Cana of Galilee.	5	A raven.

ROUND 2

	Team 1		Team 2
1	Matchbox labels.	1	Rodents.
2	Deng Xiaoping.	2	Chris Patten.
3	Mae West.	3	Shirley MacLaine.
4	Monday.	4	High-Rise.
5	A crocodile.	5	A beetle.

ROUND 3

	Team 1		Team 2
1	Sancho Panza.	1	Windmills.
2	*Aurora Borealis.*	2	Jupiter, Saturn, Uranus and Neptune.
3	Leonardo da Vinci.	3	Horses.
4	The throat.	4	To test colour vision, including the absence of it.
5	Caramel.	5	Mulligatawny.

ROUND 4

	Team 1		Team 2
1	Boeing B29 Superfortress.	1	Vickers.
2	My struggle.	2	Our affair.
3	Claude Debussy.	3	Frederick Delius.

4 Peso.
5 Chile.

4 Maltese lira.
5 The Caucasus.

ROUND 5
Soccer
Arsenal.
Famous women
The Princess Royal.
Name the year
1914.

Nature
The shamrock.
Spelling
Pseudonym.

Team 2

Team 1

ROUND 6
1 St Mark.
2 A (louse) fly.
3 Ferdinand and Isabella.
4 A clutch.
5 Khartoum.

1 St Christopher.
2 A herbaceous plant.
3 Spain or Portugal.
4 A host.
5 Tirana.

ROUND 7
1 Australian and New Zealand Army Corps.

2 *Mansfield Park*.
3 Johnny Cash.
4 Tintagel.
5 *Are You Being Served?*

1 Electronic Random Number Indicator Equipment.

2 Mr Rochester.
3 Paul McCartney.
4 King Arthur.
5 *Bread*.

ROUND 8
1 Cumberland Gap.
2 Joseph Stalin.
3 A long-sleeved coat worn loose.

4 The Netherlands.
5 The Penny Post.

1 Aiguille Verte.
2 Schicklgruber.
3 A strip of cloth wound spirally around the leg as protection.
4 Catalan.
5 Boxing gloves.

ROUND 9

1 Chicago.
2 Harriet Harman.

3 P.I. Tchaikovsky.
4 Morris Garages.
5 National Aeronautics and Space Administration.

1 Oregon.
2 The Trotter family (*Only Fools and Horses*).
3 Claude Debussy.
4 Tachometer.
5 European Space Agency.

ROUND 10
Soccer
Bertie Mee.
Famous women
Sheila Van Damm.
Name the year
1960.

Nature
Rhododendron.
Spelling
Pharyngitis.

Team 1

Team 2

DRINKS ROUND

1 A cartographer.
2 The Bass Strait.
3 Georges Braque.
4 Dallas.
5 Blue blooded (veins show blue under very white skin).
6 Ferdinand Magellan.
7 Sophia Loren.
8 Bobby Sands.
9 Testatrix.
10 Photography.

1 An ornithologist.
2 New York City.
3 Camden Town.
4 Miami.
5 El Dorado.

6 The Crimean War.
7 Candice Bergen.
8 Trevor Lock.
9 Ogress.
10 Patrick Lichfield.

RESERVE QUESTIONS

1 Gigot.
2 An apple.
3 *Hamlet*.

Pub League Quiz 2 Answers

Team 1 | Team 2

ROUND 1

Team 1	Team 2
1 Coco the Clown.	1 Jack Benny.
2 Marmalade sandwiches.	2 Cinderella.
3 *Calypso*.	3 *Mary Rose*.
4 Black.	4 Tit-tat-toe.
5 Food and Agricultural Organisation (of the United Nations).	5 Rome.

ROUND 2

Team 1	Team 2
1 Quentin Crisp.	1 Mia Farrow.
2 Saudi Arabia.	2 The Dalai Lama's.
3 A salmon.	3 An (Indian) buffalo.
4 A famous encyclopaedia.	4 *Encyclopaedia Britannica*.
5 Dinar.	5 Spain (eight reales).

ROUND 3

Team 1	Team 2
1 Geoffrey Rush (*Shine*).	1 *A Streetcar Named Desire*.
2 Prophecies.	2 'The fear of the Lord'.
3 Louisa M. Alcott.	3 *Far from the Madding Crowd*.
4 None.	4 Mars.
5 The crocus.	5 A *bouquet garni*.

ROUND 4

Team 1	Team 2
1 Lake Superior.	1 Chicago.
2 *In the Heat of the Night*.	2 *Little Caesar*.
3 Italy.	3 Operation Barbarossa.
4 *Henry V*, Act III, Scene III.	4 Verona.
5 Portsmouth harbour.	5 Buxton.

ROUND 5
Books
Georges Simenon.
Also known as
Zorro.
Characters
Sir Galahad.

Time
Sixteenth century.
Pot luck
The Niger.

A
2

Team 2   **Team 1**

ROUND 6
1 Ice figure skating (pairs).
2 On the coast of County Antrim, Northern Ireland.
3 The colour black.
4 The whale shark.
5 Letchworth.

1 Ice figure skating (individual).
2 Liverpool.

3 Nelson Mandela.
4 Bats and owls.
5 Horse Guards.

ROUND 7
1 Carbon monoxide.
2 Early golf balls.
3 Birds.
4 The fruit of the poor lemon.
5 Bonnie Prince Charlie (Prince Charles Edward Stuart).

1 Ne.
2 Curling.
3 Four.
4 Through the streets of London.
5 Switzerland.

ROUND 8
1 C.S. Lewis.
2 *Dot*.
3 St Moritz.
4 The English Channel.
5 Madame Butterfly.

1 *Peyton Place*.
2 *Levée*.
3 Norwegian.
4 Monaco.
5 *The Magic Flute*.

ROUND 9

1	Raymond Chandler.	1	Ian Ogilvy.
2	The wandering albatross.	2	Two.
3	Real Madrid.	3	Geoff Hurst.
4	George I.	4	Benjamin Britten.
5	Zorba the Greek.	5	Edgar Allan Poe.

ROUND 10

Books

Alexandre Dumas (*fils*).

Also known as

Michael Caine.

Characters

A flying school.

Time

Julius Caesar.

Pot luck

Plymouth.

Team 1

DRINKS ROUND

1 Mexican.
2 South China Sea.
3 Eric Liddell.
4 *Bleak House*.
5 *The Trouble with Harry*.
6 Lord Lucan.
7 'Oh, East is East and West is West'.
8 23.
9 Franz Beckenbauer.
10 Venezuela.

RESERVE QUESTIONS

1 Winifred Atwell.
2 Dolly.
3 A woman scorned.

Team 2

1 Belgian.
2 Madagascar.
3 *The Full Monty*.
4 *Pride and Prejudice*.
5 Sam Goldwyn.
6 John Stonehouse.
7 James Thurber.
8 Never.
9 Johan Cruyff.
10 Angels Falls (in Venezuela).

Pub League Quiz 3 Answers

Team 1

ROUND 1
1 Herman Wouk.
2 30 November.
3 *Moby Dick*.
4 He invented the flush toilet.
5 A computer which beat world champion Garry Kasparov.

ROUND 2
1 Darwin.
2 *Kismet*.
3 Demon eyes.
4 Sir Terence Conran.
5 M69.

ROUND 3
1 Sammy Davis Jnr.
2 John F. Kennedy.
3 A cat.
4 *Mauritania*.
5 Roulette.

ROUND 4
1 Lurch.
2 Four.
3 Zurich.
4 Nevil Shute.
5 Gioacchino Rossini.

Team 2

ROUND 1
1 Colleen McCullough.
2 17 March.
3 *Twelfth Night*.
4 The Bo or Bodhi tree.
5 A swimming pool.

ROUND 2
1 A missionary.
2 *Four Weddings and a Funeral*.
3 The Ombudsman.
4 Landscapes and gardens.
5 Turin.

ROUND 3
1 Bob Hope.
2 James Monroe. The capital is Monrovia.
3 Bounce.
4 *United States*.
5 15.

ROUND 4
1 Morocco.
2 Syncopate.
3 Kentucky.
4 G.K. Chesterton.
5 Karl Marx.

ROUND 5

Pop music
David Soul.

Astronomy
The corona.

Drink
A Bloody Mary.

Motor sports
Graham Hill.

Land animals
The rattlesnake.

Team 2   **Team 1**

ROUND 6

1 All are Welsh born.
2 W.A. Mozart.
3 The Berlin Wall.
4 Graham Greene.
5 The ostrich.

1 The Czech Republic.
2 P. I. Tchaikovsky.
3 He became Pope.
4 Lord Peter Wimsey.
5 The kiwi.

ROUND 7

1 FIFA.
2 Singapore.
3 *Straw Dogs*.
4 The Gettysburg Address.
5 Franz Kafka.

1 Jules Rimet.
2 Arnhem.
3 *The Graduate*.
4 Béla Bartók.
5 Thomas Mann.

ROUND 8

1 Michael Crawford.
2 Georgi Malenkov.
3 Chinese.
4 Copenhagen (the Olsen Clock in the Town Hall).
5 The Atlantic.

1 Twiggy.
2 Andrew Johnson.
3 Spanish.
4 Salisbury Cathedral.
5 The Maldive Islands.

ROUND 9

1 Kublai Khan.
2 Robert Wagner.
3 Romulus.
4 Palaeontology.
5 Lake Ontario.

1 The North-west Passage.
2 Jill Esmond.
3 Friday. After Frig.
4 Ecology.
5 The USA/Mexico border.

ROUND 10

Pop music
The Three Degrees.
Astronomy
Pluto.
Drink
Dom Pérignon.

Motor sport
Jackie Stewart.
Land animals
The giraffe.

A
3

Team 1

DRINKS ROUND

1 W.C. Fields.
2 An alcoholic.
3 Gloucestershire.
4 Honolulu.

5 Alcoholics Anonymous.
6 Edward Lear.
7 A vacuum.
8 *Haka*.
9 India.
10 A body.

RESERVE QUESTIONS
1 The last king of Albania.
2 Blackbird.
3 A lettuce.

Team 2

1 *A Day at the Races*.
2 The liver.
3 Sir Donald Bradman.
4 Rainer Werner Fassbinder.
5 One quarter.
6 Maine.
7 As an anaesthetic.
8 Cardiff City.
9 Tibet.
10 Murphy's law.

Pub League Quiz 4 Answers

Team 1

ROUND 1
1 The Black Sea.
2 Papillon.
3 The Curia.
4 *Bismarck*.
5 Sumo wrestling.

ROUND 2
1 Edwin Lutyens.
2 Night watchman and keeper of the dog pound.
3 *Oliver Twist*.
4 Pommel.
5 Roald Amundsen.

ROUND 3
1 Kissing hands.
2 Frances de la Tour.
3 J.R.R. Tolkien.
4 Royal National Lifeboat Institution.
5 Dwight D. Eisenhower.

ROUND 4
1 Rome.
2 1922 (as the British Broadcasting Company).
3 George V (of the future Edward VIII).
4 Lieutenant-colonel.
5 Charles Baudelaire.

Team 2

ROUND 1
1 Belgium.
2 Voltaire.
3 The Pope.
4 Malta.
5 Stephen Hendry.

ROUND 2
1 Harewood House.
2 Beagle.
3 Jack Dawkins.
4 Japanese.
5 Howard Carter.

ROUND 3
1 Tammany Hall.
2 Glynis Barber.
3 Emily Brontë.
4 North Atlantic Treaty Organisation.
5 Nikita Khrushchev.

ROUND 4
1 Turkey.
2 1923.
3 Ireland.
4 Wing-commander.
5 Molière.

ROUND 5

TV and radio
Charles Hill.
Ships
Savannah.
Geography
Hawaii.

Classical music
Peter and the Wolf.
Kings and queens
Persia.

Team 2	Team 1

ROUND 6

	Team 2		Team 1
1	James Hanratty.	1	Hangman.
2	Eric Cantona.	2	Jean-Paul Sartre.
3	The red fox.	3	The red deer.
4	Gammer.	4	Votaress.
5	French.	5	American.

ROUND 7

1	Weatherfield.	1	Bristol.
2	Gulf of Lions.	2	New Zealand.
3	David Bailey.	3	Gianni Versace.
4	Louise Brooks.	4	Lucky Luciano.
5	Laurence Olivier.	5	Katharine Hepburn.

ROUND 8

1	Gospel of St Mark.	1	Androcles.
2	Woods and fields, or shepherds and their flocks (either answer acceptable).	2	Hermes or Zeus (either answer acceptable).
3	Deep extra cover.	3	The Oval.
4	Glassmaker.	4	Goldsmith and jeweller.
5	Let it stand.	5	Defender of the Faith *(Fidei Defensor).*

ROUND 9

1	Dee.	1	Aberdeen.
2	The Duke of Windsor.	2	Margaret Thatcher.

3 Mount Rushmore, South Dakota.	**3** Washington, Jefferson, Lincoln and Theodore Roosevelt.
4 Cat.	**4** Rimmer.
5 Wembley stadium.	**5** The Winter Olympics.

ROUND 10
TV and radio
In the 1930s in the USA they were radio serials sponsored by soap manufacturers.
Ships
Graf Spee.
Geography
Morocco.

Classical music
W.A. Mozart.
Kings and queens
Poland.

Team 1

DRINKS ROUND
1 Dustin Hoffman.
2 An asiatic wild ox.
3 Thomas, Oliver and Richard.
4 Lord Chancellor.
5 Charles Dickens.
6 Off the coast of Norway.
7 Tina Turner.
8 Six.
9 Borstal.
10 Deep blue.

RESERVE QUESTIONS
1 Snoopy.
2 Bell ringing.
3 The Lady of Shalott.

Team 2

1 Mrs Robinson.
2 A small bird.
3 Archbishop of Canterbury.
4 Lord Chief Justice.
5 Norman Mailer.
6 Lodz.
7 Bill Wyman.
8 Six and 13.
9 Albert Desalvo.
10 Graphite.

Pub League Quiz 5 Answers

Team 1

ROUND 1
1 Dog rose.
2 Blenny.
3 Mohammed.
4 Taj Mahal.
5 Jellystone National Park.

ROUND 2
1 Nelson Eddy.
2 Dante Alighieri.
3 Suez Canal.
4 Narcissus.
5 Prince Andrew.

ROUND 3
1 Obstetrics (do not allow gynaecology).
2 Henley Royal Regatta.
3 W.A. Mozart.
4 Sir Alexander Fleming.
5 Bachelor of Dental Surgery.

ROUND 4
1 Anthony Booth.
2 The root of the marshmallow plant.
3 The Tropic of Cancer.
4 Joel Chandler Harris.
5 John Wilkes Booth.

Team 2

ROUND 1
1 Blackberries.
2 Koala bear.
3 Medina.
4 New York.
5 Peter Plant.

ROUND 2
1 Bette Davis.
2 Alfred, Lord Tennyson.
3 Caledonian Canal.
4 Castor and Pollux.
5 Cousin.

ROUND 3
1 Genealogy.
2 Korea.
3 Gioacchino Rossini.
4 Gabriel Fahrenheit.
5 Bachelor of Civil Law.

ROUND 4
1 Dandy Nicholls.
2 A biennial.
3 The Khyber Pass.
4 Thomas Hardy.
5 Ulysses S. Grant.

A
5

ROUND 5

History and warfare
Leipzig.
Law
The legal right to use land belonging to another for a particular purpose, e.g. access or drainage.

Pot luck
An army rifle.
Literature
Christopher Marlowe.
Words
Coven.

Team 2	*Team 1*

A 5

ROUND 6

1	A carat.	1	The international nautical mile.
2	Joe Louis.	2	An actress of the silent films.
3	Princess Margaret.	3	Winston Churchill.
4	Shropshire.	4	The Lizard.
5	Dibley.	5	*Blackadder.*

ROUND 7

1	Amy Lowell.	1	William Blake.
2	A scaly anteater.	2	A duck.
3	The Oval.	3	France (1906).
4	The Royal Mint.	4	A potter.
5	Rotterdam.	5	Rhine and Ruhr.

ROUND 8

1	Calliope, Clio, Urania, Terpsichore, Thalia, Euterpe, Erato, Melpomene, Polyhymnia.	1	Epic poetry and eloquence, history, astronomy, choral song and dance, comedy, lyric poetry and music, love poetry and music, tragedy, sacred poetry and music.
2	1823 (at Rugby School).	2	1871.
3	William II.	3	Richard I.
4	Pottery fired but not glazed.	4	An old Chinese glaze, greyish to blue-green.

5 November 1899–
February 1900.

5 1627–28.

ROUND 9
1 Voltaire.
2 The liver.
3 Cleopatra (VII of Egypt).
4 St Paul's Cathedral.
5 *The Great Dictator* (1940).

1 Samuel Johnson.
2 The gums.
3 Alexander the Great.
4 Canterbury Cathedral.
5 *Santa Fé Trail*.

ROUND 10
History and warfare
Yalta in the Crimea.
Law
Quarter sessions.
Pot luck
Iraq.

Literature
'A gentleman'.
Words
Numismatics.

A
5

Team 1

Team 2

DRINKS ROUND
1 William Hague.
2 1979.
3 Blaise Pascal.
4 A farthingale.
5 Mahon.
6 Terence Rattigan.
7 Georges.
8 Her (His) Majesty's
Stationery Office.

9 A wading bird (a white
heron).
10 Carbuncle.

1 Andre Agassi.
2 Walter Mondale.
3 John Knox.
4 A glengarry.
5 Somalia.
6 T.S. Eliot.
7 Arthur.
8 Associated Society of
Locomotive Engineers
and Firemen.
9 A small duck.
10 Your lungs.

RESERVE QUESTIONS
1 It was the test site for
the first atomic bomb.

2 A Copenhagen Mary.
3 Detached from one
another.

Pub League Quiz 6 Answers

Team 1

ROUND 1
1   Lhasa, Tibet.

2   Italy.
3   St Stephen, Vienna.
4   William the Conqueror.
5   19.

ROUND 2
1   St Albans.
2   D.I.V.O.R.C.E.
3   J. M. Barrie.
4   Johann Strauss (the Younger).
5   Gymnasium.

ROUND 3
1   International Business Machines.
2   John McCarthy and Brian Keenan.
3   The book or text of the performance.
4   Flemish (Belgian).
5   Jack the Ripper.

ROUND 4
1   Quakers.
2   Peter O'Toole.
3   Kenya.
4   Laudanum.
5   Nuremberg.

Team 2

ROUND 1
1   Queensland and Northern Territory Airline Service.
2   Lourdes.
3   St Mark's.
4   French.
5   31.

ROUND 2
1   Marston Moor.
2   Village People.
3   *Peter Pan.*
4   The bat.
5   Pistol shooting.

ROUND 3
1   International Monetary Fund.
2   Edward Elgar.
3   When the whole text is sung.
4   American.
5   10 Rillington Place.

ROUND 4
1   *Zen.*
2   Jack Nicholson.
3   Hawaii.
4   Mescalin.
5   The Bayeux tapestry.

A
6

ROUND 5
History
George V.
Entertainment
The Comedy of Errors.
Animals
A beautifully coloured fish.

Literature
The Book of the Dead.
Aircraft
Frank Whittle.

Team 2	Team 1

ROUND 6

Team 2
1 Wightman Cup.
2 Istanbul.
3 See opposite question and answer.

4 Genera.
5 By means of flowing water.

Team 1
1 Kentucky Derby.
2 Milan.
3 Catherine of Aragon, Anne Boleyn, Jane Seymour, Anne of Cleves, Catherine Howard and Catherine Parr.
4 Geneses.
5 Raising water.

ROUND 7

Team 2
1 The Seekers.
2 Royal Horse Artillery.

3 Coventry City.
4 Winfield.
5 Andy Warhol.

Team 1
1 Elvis Presley.
2 Royal Electrical and Mechanical Engineers.
3 Preston North End.
4 Selfridges.
5 Goldie Hawn.

ROUND 8

Team 2
1 A beetle.
2 Edgar Wallace.
3 River Kabul.
4 Paris.
5 Knee cartilage.

Team 1
1 Deathwatch beetle.
2 Mrs Gaskell.
3 Zaire.
4 The Minotaur.
5 The female breast.

ROUND 9

1	Traffic lights.	1	Alfred Nobel.
2	Karl Malden and Michael Douglas.	2	Steve Garrett.
3	Martin Luther King.	3	Germany.
4	Paprika.	4	Nutmeg.
5	Claude-Joseph Rouget de Lisle.	5	Japan's.

ROUND 10

History
Portuguese.
Entertainment
Dustin Hoffman and John Voight.
Animals
The mute swan.

Literature
The Fellowship of the Ring; The Two Towers; The Return of the King.
Aircraft
Mach 2.

Team 1

DRINKS ROUND
1 *The Rivals.*
2 Tony Randall.
3 They are all Canadian rivers.
4 Jodie Foster.
5 Edinburgh.
6 Pembrokeshire coast.
7 Donald Sinden and Windsor Davies.
8 Arnold Bennett.
9 Lascar.
10 Molars.

Team 2

1 Walter de la Mare.
2 James Cagney.
3 They were all Astronomers Royal.
4 Theresa Russell.
5 Schoolmaster.
6 The Lake District.
7 *Soap.*
8 Pathfinder Bennett.
9 A gold prospector.
10 Incisors.

RESERVE QUESTIONS
1 *Christ.*
2 Dr Samuel Johnson.
3 Polyandry.

Pub League Quiz 7 Answers

Team 1

ROUND 1
1 Paul Henry.
2 US Grand Prix.
3 1,000.
4 1376.
5 Bow Bells (St Mary-le-Bow).

ROUND 2
1 Norway and Sweden.
2 A lullaby.
3 The middle price.
4 *Marriage à la Mode*.
5 29 September.

ROUND 3
1 Pudding Lane (near the north end of London Bridge).
2 John Milton.
3 Linda Gray.
4 Magnesium hydroxide.
5 An animal with a pouch.

ROUND 4
1 Medina.
2 A circus acrobat.
3 Norman Tebbit's.
4 Easter Island.
5 Breeds of chicken.

Team 2

1 King's Oak.
2 US Masters (golf).
3 12.
4 Set in the Imperial State Crown.
5 Cheapside.

1 Oslo.
2 A Hindu nurse or ladies' maid.
3 Cost, Insurance, Freight.
4 Pablo Picasso.
5 The feast of St Michael and All Angels.

1 To commemorate the Great Fire of London.
2 *Paradise Regained*.
3 Patrick Duffy.
4 Amphetamines.
5 The elephant.

1 *Muezzin*.
2 *Easy Rider*.
3 Lloyd's of London.
4 Australia's.
5 Breeds of sheep.

ROUND 5
Pop music
Davy Jones.
Children's books
Lewis Carroll *(Through the Looking-Glass and what Alice found there)*.

Classical music
Franz Lehár *(The Merry Widow)*.
Pot luck
A knot.
History
Peter I (the Great).

Team 2

Team 1

ROUND 6
1 Leo Tolstoy.
2 In secret.
3 The Cavern Club.
4 Alternative Investment Market.

5 Australia.

1 Alexander Pushkin.
2 By the grace of God.
3 The Hollies.
4 Home Office Large Major Enquiry System (the police national database of criminal records).

5 Uganda.

ROUND 7
1 Palindrome.

2 The Crystal Palace.
3 Norwegian.
4 Mozambique.
5 Christopher Fry.

1 A line of verse of two measures.
2 Queen Victoria.
3 Sonja.
4 Surinam.
5 Alan Bennett.

ROUND 8
1 Raphael.
2 Valhalla.
3 Newport County.
4 Hudson.
5 Fellow of the Royal Society of Arts.

1 Michelangelo.
2 Jupiter (or Jove).
3 West Bromwich Albion.
4 Wendy Craig.
5 Fellow of the Royal College of Music.

ROUND 9
1 Thrift.

1 Aubretia.

2	Australia.	2	Colorado.
3	W. Somerset Maugham.	3	John Steinbeck.
4	William Gladstone.	4	Sir Henry Campbell-Bannerman.
5	Balboa.	5	Koruna.

ROUND 10
Pop music
Ginger, Scary, Posh, Baby and Sporty.

Classical music
The 'Hallelujah Chorus' from Handel's *Messiah*.

Children's books
McTurk and Beetle.

Pot luck
Pollen.

History
Antigone.

Team 1

Team 2

DRINKS ROUND

1	Gravity, that is, usually the constant of gravitation in Newton's Law.	1	Joule.
2	The Fosse Way.	2	Watling Street.
3	Turkey.	3	Belize.
4	Modest Mussorgsky.	4	Richard Wagner.
5	Ernie Bishop.	5	Alf Roberts.
6	D. H. Lawrence.	6	Frederick Forsyth.
7	European Free Trade Association.	7	London and North Eastern Railway.
8	The murdered Edward V and his brother Richard, Duke of York.	8	Louis XVIII.
9	Trevor Howard.	9	Jane Seymour.
10	'A fine lady upon a white horse'.	10	A pieman.

RESERVE QUESTIONS

| 1 | A straight furrow. | 3 | Whooping cough. |
| 2 | Tasmanian tiger (thylacine). | | |

Pub League Quiz 8 Answers

Team 1	Team 2

ROUND 1

	Team 1		Team 2
1	Daphne du Maurier.	1	John Steinbeck.
2	Franz Joseph Haydn.	2	Edward Elgar.
3	Lusaka.	3	Muscat.
4	Like a woman.	4	Mother-of-pearl.
5	James Stewart.	5	James Stewart.

ROUND 2

	Team 1		Team 2
1	De Havilland.	1	Lockheed.
2	Pasta shapes.	2	Peppers, aubergines, courgettes, onions.
3	30.	3	The Crystal Palace.
4	Oxygen.	4	A storm.
5	Raymond Chandler.	5	Arthur Conan Doyle.

ROUND 3

	Team 1		Team 2
1	Ruth Madoc.	1	Betty Driver.
2	Matt Biondi.	2	Men's hockey.
3	Alexander Pope.	3	Franklin D. Roosevelt.
4	*Top of the Pops*.	4	At Prestwick airport.
5	Zion.	5	Turkey.

ROUND 4

	Team 1		Team 2
1	St Dunstan.	1	St Nicholas.
2	A beetle.	2	A snake.
3	National Film Theatre.	3	*The Financial Times*.
4	Prince Charles.	4	14 June.
5	Valéry Giscard d'Estaing.	5	Lord Palmerston.

A
8

ROUND 5
Sport
Sabre.
Soap operas
Colorado.
England
Oxford.

Science
Archimedes.
Art
Velasquez.

Team 2	**Team 1**

ROUND 6

1	West Germany.	**1**	An ice skater.
2	Ray Milland.	**2**	Spencer Tracy.
3	Lesotho.	**3**	Zambia.
4	Lord Beaverbrook.	**4**	Leon Trotsky.
5	Rabbits.	**5**	Alexander Selkirk.

ROUND 7

1	An Australian bird (kookaburra).	**1**	A large antelope.
2	A sweet-scented garden plant.	**2**	Damson.
3	Bad law.	**3**	Kavanagh QC.
4	Old Deuteronomy.	**4**	Revelations.
5	Australia.	**5**	Fangio, Farina and Fagioli.

ROUND 8

1	John Nash.	**1**	Frank Lloyd Wright.
2	Steve Biko.	**2**	*Cry Freedom*.
3	*Strike it Lucky*.	**3**	Arthur Askey.
4	Nikolai Gogol.	**4**	John Osborne.
5	Cornell.	**5**	Bismarck.

ROUND 9

1	Margaret Smith.	1	Jimmy White.
2	Vice-admiral.	2	Lieutenant.
3	Memphis, Tennessee.	3	John Connolly.
4	Glasgow.	4	Birmingham.
5	Cecil B. de Mille.	5	John Ford.

ROUND 10

Sport
Women's tennis.
Soap operas
Laura Palmer.
England
Wardour Street.

Science
Quantum theory.
Art
John Everett Millais.

Team 1

DRINKS ROUND
1 *The Mikado*.
2 Abba.
3 Whit Sunday.
4 Spring.
5 Lily of the valley.
6 Port Said.
7 William Butler Yeats.
8 Holland.
9 Bob Hoskins.
10 Romulus.

Team 2

1 *The Pirates of Penzance*.
2 Crystal Gayle.
3 He performed miracles.
4 Witches.
5 Forget-me-not.
6 Lakes Erie and Ontario.
7 James Cain.
8 Belgium.
9 *Godspell*.
10 The Appian Way.

RESERVE QUESTIONS
1 1752.
2 Hormones.
3 Grandfather and grandson.

A
8

Pub League Quiz 9 Answers

Team 1

ROUND 1
1 *Ben Hur.*
2 Clement Attlee.
3 Madrid.
4 Somerset.
5 A bird.

ROUND 2
1 James Brown.
2 Wind speed.

3 'Jabberwocky'.
4 The difference in pitch between two notes.
5 St Teresa of Avila.

ROUND 3
1 *Barbarella.*
2 A form.
3 Britain and China.
4 Antonio.
5 Honolulu.

ROUND 4
1 Gerald Ford.
2 Kitty Kelley.
3 Ten dollars.
4 David Livingstone.
5 15 July.

Team 2

1 Katharine Hepburn.
2 Jo Grimond.
3 Washington.
4 Salop.
5 The weasel family.

1 Aretha Franklin.
2 Many voiced, or represented by different sounds.
3 The slithy toves.
4 A semitone.

5 St James (Jaime).

1 *Love Me Tender.*
2 An eyrie.
3 USA.
4 Othello.
5 Sacramento.

1 James Callaghan.
2 Andrew Morton.
3 A monkey.
4 India.
5 May.

A
9

ROUND 5
Television
A Question of Sport.
Classical music
The Four Seasons.
Law
Hilary, Easter, Trinity and
Michaelmas.

General knowledge
Robert Maxwell.
Nicknames
Vinegar Joe.

Team 2 | **Team 1**

ROUND 6
1 Louth.
2 Sonny and Cher.
3 Ironsides.
4 Proper names.
5 Mead.

1 Kildare.
2 Anton Karas.
3 Beefeaters.
4 Belief in one god.
5 A large wine bottle.

ROUND 7
1 Neptune.
2 *The Flying Dutchman.*
3 'The Knight's Tale'.
4 A long nose.
5 Essex.

1 Neptune.
2 Merlin.
3 'The Parson's Tale'.
4 Australia.
5 The Royal Hospital,
   Chelsea.

ROUND 8
1 Maize.
2 Chronus.
3 Lionel Bart.
4 Irving Stone.
5 The inability to stay
   awake.

1 Malt.
2 Saturn.
3 *Paint Your Wagon.*
4 Sax Rohmer.
5 Aspirin.

A
9

ROUND 9

1 H.M.S. *Hood*.

2 Edinburgh.
3 Leopold I (1831–1865).
4 Marcus Sargeant.
5 Audi.

1 It was sunk by a German submarine.
2 *The Morning Star*.
3 Robert II (1371–1390).
4 Pope John Paul II.
5 Estée Lauder.

ROUND 10

Television
Private Godfrey.
Classical music
Mikhail Glinka.
Law
Jurisprudence.

General knowledge
New York.
Nicknames
Sandro Botticelli.

Team 1

Team 2

DRINKS ROUND

1 Chile.
2 True.
3 Racehorse training.
4 Benedictine.

5 Fountains Abbey.
6 *It's That Man Again*.
7 Jersey Joe Walcott.
8 Derek McCulloch.
9 Northumberland.
10 Hilda.

1 A geyser.
2 True.
3 Cycle racing.
4 Sweetened spiced wine with hot water.
5 Whipsnade Zoo.
6 Will Hay.
7 Gracie Fields.
8 Vera Lynn.
9 Somerset.
10 Harold Macmillan.

RESERVE QUESTIONS

1 The Duke of Wellington and Sir Winston Churchill.
2 Barbados.
3 Walt Disney (e.g. *Fantasia*).

A 9

Pub League Quiz 10 Answers

Team 1

ROUND 1
1 Paternoster.
2 France.
3 1966.
4 Schoolmaster.
5 22.

ROUND 2
1 Commonwealth Day and the birthday of Prince Edward.
2 Oasis.
3 The peacock.
4 John Churchill.
5 Contract bridge.

ROUND 3
1 33 and 21.
2 Gozo or Comino.
3 Captain Matthew Webb.
4 Rotherham United.
5 James II.

ROUND 4
1 Entirely or completely.
2 John Reith.
3 Ouse.
4 Archery.
5 Poland.

Team 2

1 165.
2 Argentina.
3 Queen Victoria.
4 Lawyer.
5 Bagatelle.

1 Albert, Caroline and Stephanie.
2 Hale and Pace.
3 The phoenix.
4 Blenheim.
5 Canoeing.

1 15 and 5.
2 Paraguay.
3 Polo.
4 Liverpool, Middlesborough, Sampdoria.
5 Carolingians.

1 That is (i.e.).
2 Learie Constantine.
3 Nid.
4 Sagittarius.
5 Hungary.

A 10

ROUND 5

In common
They were all American presidents.

Name the year
1948.

Pop music
Mariah Carey.

Religion
Wassailing.

Pot luck
The Bishop of Bath and Wells.

Team 2   **Team 1**

ROUND 6

	Team 2		Team 1
1	By rubbing its wing covers together.	1	By flapping its wings very rapidly.
2	The Organisation of African Unity.	2	National Farmers' Union.
3	Sussex.	3	Wilton House.
4	Accolade.	4	The Abbey Theatre.
5	A legless lizard.	5	Mammals.

ROUND 7

	Team 2		Team 1
1	Audrey Roberts.	1	Benson.
2	*Fesse*.	2	*Gardant*.
3	Alexander Dumas (*père*).	3	W. Somerset Maugham.
4	*Tass*.	4	Vichy.
5	Greyfriars.	5	Uncle Remus.

A 10

ROUND 8

	Team 2		Team 1
1	St Lawrence.	1	Arizona.
2	Pigeons or doves.	2	Dingo.
3	John Adams.	3	George Washington.
4	A boar.	4	Dido.
5	Hobart.	5	Bucharest.

ROUND 9

1	William Wordsworth.	1	John Masefield.
2	The Battle of Crécy.	2	Richard I (Richard the Lionheart).
3	The Ten Commandments.	3	The Gospels.
4	Cassava roots.	4	Wheat.
5	Catalyst.	5	Nitrogen.

ROUND 10

In common
Ballet.
Name the year
1968.
Pop music
Cat Stevens.

Religion
The Wailing Wall in Jerusalem.
Pot luck
George Bernard Shaw.

Team 1

Team 2

DRINKS ROUND

1	*Guys and Dolls*.	1	*Pal Joey*.
2	Southern Crown and Northern Crown.	2	It always points away from the sun.
3	James Earl Ray.	3	Nathuram Godse.
4	Small holes that let water run off the deck.	4	A rail across or round the stern of the boat.
5	1300 hrs (1 p.m.).	5	0700 hrs (7 a.m.).
6	Albrecht Dürer.	6	Lucas Cranach.
7	Milky-bluish.	7	Heliotrope.
8	Infinite knowledge, all knowing.	8	A name made up of initial letters, e.g. ERNIE.
9	December.	9	Messalina.
10	Ben Kingsley.	10	Liza Minnelli.

RESERVE QUESTIONS
1 A tenor.
2 Brendan Behan.
3 Fabrizio Ravanelli.

A
10

Pub League Quiz 11 Answers

Team 1

ROUND 1
1 Sun Hill.
2 Finland.
3 Douglas Adams.
4 Royal Australian Air Force.
5 New York.

ROUND 2
1 *The Treasure of Sierra Madre* (Walter Huston).
2 Grandson.
3 Betty Grable.
4 Hydrogen.
5 Ambrosia.

ROUND 3
1 Lord Carrington.
2 Pickled cabbage.
3 *Tommy.*
4 Lucy Honeychurch.
5 I play.

ROUND 4
1 Humber, Thames, Severn and Mersey.
2 France.
3 John the Baptist.
4 Haemophilia.
5 Civet.

Team 2

ROUND 1
1 Warmington-on-Sea.
2 Charles Stewart Parnell.
3 Terence Stamp.
4 Chief of the General Staff.
5 Stalingrad.

ROUND 2
1 Woody Allen.
2 Two. William II and Henry I.
3 Marilyn Monroe.
4 Helium.
5 Nectar.

ROUND 3
1 Denis Healey.
2 *Scampo.*
3 Scott Joplin.
4 Mince and slices of quince.
5 Six.

ROUND 4
1 Scafell Pike, Ben Nevis, Snowdon and Carrantuohill.
2 Georgia.
3 River Jordan.
4 Sleeping sickness.
5 USA.

A
11

ROUND 5
Films
Live and Let Die.
Plants and wildlife
A type of grass.
Dates
2000.

Sport
Georges Carpentier.
General knowledge
Brown Owl.

Team 2   *Team 1*

ROUND 6
1 *David Copperfield* and *Great Expectations.*
2 Nine.
3 The fear of public or open places.
4 Harry Secombe.
5 Cardale.

1 Bootsie and Snudge.
2 Economics.
3 An all-consuming passion for power.
4 Dorothy Parker.
5 Annette Crosbie.

ROUND 7
1 Finland.
2 The world professional darts championship.
3 P.
4 *The Prince and the Showgirl.*
5 Orkney.

1 Paraguay.
2 Peter Scudamore.
3 Bauxite.
4 *Lawrence of Arabia.*
5 Lewis.

ROUND 8
1 1948.
2 Manchester.
3 Jack Johnson.
4 'Elegy Written in a Country Churchyard' (Thomas Gray).
5 North and South Korea.

1 King George VI.
2 Lace-making.
3 Joe Bugner.
4 'The Soldier' (Rupert Brooke).
5 USA and Canada.

A
11

ROUND 9

1 Charles I.
2 Cliff Richard.
3 *Goodbye Mr Chips*.

4 Kiel.

5 Three.

1 The Queen of Hearts.
2 Lionel Bart.
3 *The Prime of Miss Jean Brodie*.

4 The Battle of the Coral Sea.

5 88.

ROUND 10

Films
Steven Spielberg.
Plants and wildlife
The potato.
Dates
The moon.

Sport
Hamilton, Canada.
General knowledge
His amputated leg.

Team 1

Team 2

DRINKS ROUND

1 Eleanor of Acquitaine.
2 The Medway.
3 Mexico.
4 Trees.
5 Anton Chekov.
6 'Roffen'.
7 Angola.

8 Anna Ford.
9 Corsica.
10 River Elbe.

1 James I (of England).
2 The Chilterns.
3 Spain.
4 Stitches.
5 *Rigoletto*.
6 'Carliol'.
7 South America (Ecuador and Peru).
8 *Crimewatch UK*.
9 Vinci (Tuscany).
10 Afghanistan.

**A
11**

RESERVE QUESTIONS

1 The kidneys.
2 Lal Bahadour Shastri.
3 Count Basie.

Pub League Quiz 12 Answers

Team 1

ROUND 1
1 1896.
2 A locksmith.
3 *Gone with the Wind*.
4 Captain Lawrence Oates.
5 Cecilia.

ROUND 2
1 Botswana.
2 Pelé.
3 Magnesium.
4 Cleave.
5 Africa.

ROUND 3
1 Ben Jonson.
2 Advanced Passenger Train.
3 Aspirin.
4 Eight.
5 Algeria.

ROUND 4
1 A hoofed animal which chews the cud, e.g. a sheep, cow, goat, etc.
2 The Champs Elysées.
3 All Olympic 100 metres champions.
4 Puck.
5 Jean Boht.

Team 2

ROUND 1
1 Sapporo in Japan.
2 The electric razor.
3 Agatha Christie.
4 The French Resistance.
5 The Scaffold.

ROUND 2
1 India and Pakistan.
2 Squash.
3 Radium.
4 Dreamt.
5 Kenya.

ROUND 3
1 George Eliot.
2 British Army of the Rhine.
3 The cash register.
4 Two.
5 Israel.

ROUND 4
1 A beggar (or a friar of a begging order).
2 Pennsylvania Avenue.
3 Hammer.
4 Miranda in *The Tempest*.
5 Cher.

A
12

ROUND 5
Sport
Table tennis.
Art and artists
Peter.
Nobel Prize winners
Le Duc Tho (North
Vietnam).

Composers
Ralph Vaughan Williams.
English monarchs
Edward IV.

Team 2   *Team 1*

ROUND 6
1   Belgium.
2   Water.

3   Three.
4   The Netherlands.
5   *Equus*.

1   Italy (Vatican City).
2   Both on one side of its
    head.
3   Mercury.
4   Germany.
5   *The Rivals*.

ROUND 7
1   Bolivia.
2   France (1924).
3   Herring or sprats.
4   Mobiles.

5   Cambodia.

1   Caracas, Venezuela.
2   Eric Liddell.
3   Gudgeon.
4   Hudson (Hudson River
    School).
5   Mau Mau.

ROUND 8
1   *The Phil Silvers Show*.
2   Timmy, the dog.
3   John Lennon.
4   Henrik Ibsen.
5   The Rose Bowl.

1   *Till Death Us Do Part*.
2   John Mills.
3   Manila.
4   Eugene O'Neill.
5   The Orange Bowl.

A
12

ROUND 9
1   African slaves.
2   Herman Wouk.
3   John McEnroe.
4   Heinrich Hertz.

1   New Zealand.
2   Ernest Hemingway.
3   18.
4   Frederick W. Lanchester.

5 Svengali.

5 *The Inn of the Sixth Happiness*.

ROUND 10
Sport
Ice hockey.
Art and artists
Turner.
Nobel Prize winners
UNICEF.

Composers
Claudio Monteverdi's.
English monarchs
Hardicanute.

Team 1

Team 2

DRINKS ROUND
1 *The Good Old Days*.
2 The Supremes.

3 The Boat Race.
4 Bonn.
5 Hungary.
6 Mars.
7 The fox.

8 Francophile.
9 Incitatus.
10 George Orwell (in *1984*).

1 *Breakfast Time*.
2 Elaine Page and Barbara Dickson.
3 A horse race in the wet.
4 Australia.
5 Must.
6 Venus.
7 By ensuring that her prophecies were not believed.
8 The fear of eating.
9 Clyde.
10 Jonathan Swift (in *Gulliver's Travels*).

RESERVE QUESTIONS
1 Rupee.
2 Salk.
3 Plato.

A
12

Pub League Quiz 13 Answers

Team 1

ROUND 1
1 The Gulf of Mexico.
2 'Over the Hills and Far Away'.
3 William Randolph Hearst.
4 Reginald.
5 The palms of the hands or the soles of the feet.

ROUND 2
1 Ecuador.
2 *Rosemary's Baby*.
3 Everly Brothers.
4 John Dryden.
5 78 feet.

ROUND 3
1 Sikhism.
2 Jumbo.
3 Biopsy.
4 The hoping or hopeful one.
5 MM.

ROUND 4
1 Lady.
2 Turkey.
3 Leningrad (St Petersburg).
4 35 to 1.
5 Ganges.

Team 2

1 Lapland.
2 Nine days' old.
3 Christine Keeler.
4 H.G. Wells.
5 Tooth enamel.

1 Argentina.
2 *A Clockwork Orange*.
3 The Kinks.
4 'Solitude' (Ella Wheeler Wilcox).
5 Three feet.

1 Hinduism.
2 Comanche.
3 Biosphere.
4 Divine wind.
5 Zero.

1 Dame.
2 Xi'an.
3 Dame Ninette de Valois.
4 Ten.
5 Zaire.

A
13

ROUND 5

Famous people
Sculpture.
Films
Francis Coppola.
Wars
World War 2.

The Ancients
Prometheus.
Plant life
Hellebore.

Team 2

Team 1

ROUND 6

1	Lake Titicaca.
2	Jon Voight.
3	China.
4	Vincent Van Gogh.
5	Influenza.

1	Eilat.
2	Jane Fonda.
3	Belgium.
4	*Steppenwolf*.
5	Group O.

ROUND 7

1 4¼ inches.
2 Melodion.

3 Gibb.
4 Lawrence Durrell.
5 Green.

1 An air (or fresh air) shot.
2 With small wooden hammers.
3 Wilson.
4 David Storey.
5 Champagne and stout.

ROUND 8

1 Noel Edmonds.
2 Hannibal.
3 Hawaii.
4 Kitty Hawk.
5 Bullfighting.

1 A tub of lard.
2 The Persians.
3 Jay Gatsby.
4 Howard Hughes himself.
5 Shinty.

**A
13**

ROUND 9

1	Cyprus.	1	The Faeroe Islands.
2	Axl Rose (real name William Bailey).	2	Shane McGowan.
3	The storming of the Bastille.	3	Epiphany.
4	*The Colbys*.	4	Mayday.
5	Carbon dioxide.	5	454.

ROUND 10

Famous people
Ranulph Fiennes.
Films
The Exorcist.
Wars
World War 1.

The Ancients
Chinese.
Plant life
Mushroom.

Team 1

Team 2

DRINKS ROUND

1	Harold Holt.	1	Olivia Newton-John.
2	Ronnie Wood.	2	Elton John.
3	Canadian.	3	Linford Christie.
4	A Harvey Wallbanger.	4	Ginger beer.
5	George Herman.	5	John Berry.
6	Three days and three nights.	6	The *Haggadah*.
7	Tamil.	7	Malay.
8	28.	8	12.
9	Singapore.	9	The Reichstag.
10	William Shatner.	10	Derek Jacobi.

RESERVE QUESTIONS
1 The Bay of Biscay.
2 Paranoia.
3 Electric current.

A
13

Pub League Quiz 14 Answers

Team 1

ROUND 1
1 Euboea.
2 Claude Debussy.
3 Adam West.
4 Fulmar.
5 Gymnastics.

ROUND 2
1 Massachusetts.
2 Yul Brynner.
3 1,001.
4 A moorland plant.
5 Eddie Charlton.

ROUND 3
1 Lady Godiva.
2 Paul Klee.
3 Water.
4 Cycle racing.
5 China.

ROUND 4
1 Margery Allingham.
2 Oscar Hammerstein II.
3 Peter Pan.
4 Smell.
5 Mexico City.

Team 2

ROUND 1
1 Great Britain.
2 *La Traviata*.
3 Cesar Romero.
4 The chicken.
5 Straw.

ROUND 2
1 Chuck Berry.
2 Robert Carlyle.
3 Eight.
4 Cuckoo-pint.
5 Jackie and Bobby Charlton.

ROUND 3
1 Atlas.
2 Salvador Dali.
3 1/11.
4 Billiards.
5 Between Spain and Gibraltar.

ROUND 4
1 Patricia Routledge.
2 George Gershwin.
3 Rudyard Kipling.
4 The heel.
5 El Salvador.

A
14

ROUND 5

Characters
Mrs Hudson.
International affairs
Alaska.
Disasters
Tenerife.

Horses and courses
Red Rum.
Inventions
The Polaroid camera.

Team 2	Team 1

ROUND 6

1	Indiana.	1	Indonesia.
2	Wyatt Earp.	2	Audie Murphy.
3	Thaler.	3	*Cha.*
4	49.	4	20.
5	Cartilage.	5	Plankton.

ROUND 7

1	The potato.	1	Carp.
2	The British Museum.	2	The Man in the Iron Mask.
3	Neil Diamond or Donna Summer.	3	Frank and Nancy Sinatra.
4	Herbal medicine.	4	*Old Moore's Almanack.*
5	Six.	5	'Fallen Madonna with the Big Boobies'.

ROUND 8

1	Rod Steiger.	1	James Mason.
2	The cheetah.	2	The raccoon.
3	He stole a loaf of bread.	3	Barabas.
4	*Amoco Cadiz.*	4	Amnesty International.
5	Floria Tosca.	5	Franz Joseph Haydn.

A
14

ROUND 9

1 A small ship with sails and/or oars.
2 Sir Thomas More.
3 Sir Alec Douglas-Home.
4 Christina Rossetti.

5 Denmark's.

1 John Cobb.

2 Woodrow Wilson.
3 Kingston, Jamaica.
4 The nightingale (in 'Ode to a Nightingale', by Keats).
5 Lutheranism.

ROUND 10
Characters
The Salvation Army.
International affairs
The Cuban missile crisis.
Disasters
Darwin.

Horses and courses
One mile.
Inventions
Microwave oven.

Team 1

DRINKS ROUND
1 The Saint Lawrence.
2 Sussex.
3 Colonel Gaddafi.
4 *Bad Day at Black Rock*.
5 James Joyce.
6 The air gap between the cork and the wine.
7 Walter.
8 Vic Windsor.
9 Belgium.
10 Pigmy shrewmouse.

Team 2

1 The Denmark Strait.
2 Malcolm Nash.
3 Alexei Kosygin.
4 *Torn Curtain*.
5 Dylan Thomas.
6 The lees.

7 Charlie Drake.
8 Sam Failsworth.
9 In the Inner Hebrides.
10 The bandicoot.

RESERVE QUESTIONS

1 Sulphuric acid.
2 Helen Keller.
3 The House of Lords.